Humanistic Business

Humanistic Business

Profit through People
with Passion and Purpose

*Todd Hutchison, Carl Lyons
and Gary de Rodriguez*

B L O O M S B U R Y
LONDON • NEW DELHI • NEW YORK • SYDNEY

First published in Great Britain 2014

Copyright © Todd Hutchison, Carl Lyons and Gary de Rodriguez, 2014

Bloomsbury Publishing Plc
50 Bedford Square
London
WC1B 3DP

www.bloomsbury.com

Bloomsbury Publishing
London, New Delhi, New York and Sydney

A CIP record for this book is available from the British Library.

ISBN: 9-781-4729-04782

10 9 8 7 6 5 4 3 2 1

Design by Fiona Pike, Pike Design, Winchester
Typeset by Hewer Text UK Ltd, Edinburgh
Printed and bound in Great Britain by CPI Group (UK) Ltd, Croydon CR0 4YY

Contents

Acknowledgements

Todd Hutchison
I would like to acknowledge Jukka Sappinen from Extended DISC® for the use of images in this book showing his amazing and world-leading behavioural system. I would also like to recognise the great teachers who have touched me the most: Anthony Robbins, Brian Tracey, Robert Kiyosaki, Dr Wayne Dwyer, Dr Joe Dispenza and the late Jim Rohn. Lastly, those most important angels that touch my life and give me daily inspiration: my mother Dalveen, wife Gina and daughter Lara. We are all shaped by those who leave footprints on our hearts, and changed forever more.

Carl Lyons
I would like to thank my wife, Michele, for her love and support during the writing of this book. Our three beautiful daughters, Lily, Poppy and Rose, are my constant inspiration and who will occupy that future we hope to shape for the better.

Gary De Rodriguez
I would like to acknowledge Raj Sisodia for his contribution to Conscious Capitalism, as well as Robert Dilts, John Overdurf, Connie Ray Andreas and Julie Silverthorn who wielded the tools of NLP with such grace it inspired me to dive deeper into the business application of the science of human excellence. Peter Senge for his work in systems thinking. Edward De Bono for his simple and effective methods to increase perspective and flexibility in thinking. To Robert Sargeleski for his unwavering support of my career and his belief in me as a man, but most importantly for his ability to help me stay in the infinite NOW laughing.

Introduction

The business landscape is changing. Our intent in writing this book was to help create a new vision of the future for how business will be done, challenge old models and ways of thinking and contribute to the redesign of the new enterprises of tomorrow. It complements existing research that shows the profit in applying these new business principles, and it demonstrates the mechanics of how to achieve it.

We are living in times of enormous change and there is clear evidence around the world of political, social and economic unrest. We see this as part of a transformation in consciousness of many individuals, organisations, countries and cultures, ultimately evolving towards a greater awareness of our impact on other human beings and the environment in which we live. It seems that people are caring more, they are choosing to have a voice in support of humankind and are holding our governments, organisations and leaders to account so that they do more of the 'right' thing. Collectively, we are calling on leaders to contribute rather than harm, and to be more honest, open and transparent. This raised consciousness leads the drive towards modifying our behaviour and seeking new ways of being.

Global business leaders like Richard Branson are collectively saying the world is at a critical crossroads, calling on worldwide leaders to come together to advance the wellbeing of people and the planet. Greater consciousness in business is becoming the voiced solution pitched to global businesses in order to survive and thrive throughout the transition.

Although raising consciousness stimulates action and provides a desire to change, often individuals and organisations are not sure how to make the positive step into this new era of doing business. Many see the need to be more transparent, ethical and aware as being a nice idea, but if they actually behave in this way they will not be able to compete in the 'real-world'. We recognise that this may be a lofty ideal, which is why we have combined the idealism with a healthy dose of pragmatism, practical experience and industry proof of its benefits. Our aim here is to provide a model for developing an exceptional business that does great in the world. We've called this new model humanistic business as it's based on engaging with and serving not just individuals, but also contributing to the wider community.

Good relationships and serving others is what has historically underpinned the success of a business. Traditionally, business was based on bartering one's own produce with others, with each individual following their own specialisation to offer their trades to the wider community. With the arrival of the industrial age there was a shift towards the masses of workers employed by corporations, and the 'what is in it for me?' mentality of the employee. The information age places the focus on technology, which is moving more and more towards collaborative communication technologies. We are now entering the consciousness age, which will make businesses think and act about how they serve others. This does not mean a loss of focus on profit, rather a gain as a result of doing well and becoming admired for the contribution they make and the responsible way they act.

Humanistic businesses are simply those organisations which are extraordinarily self-aware. They are clear about their values and purpose and consciously set out to make a positive contribution to everything they impact upon with integrity, authenticity and transparency. They recognise the interdependence of the world we live in and operate with a view to achieving sustainability, including lasting profitability. Their model is about doing well and at the same time doing good.

Our objective for this book is to share some of the insights we've discovered through research, investigation and practical application while observing and working with businesses at the leading edge of this movement. Our goal was to dive deep into the absolute foundation and principles that lead to the more observable traits of these businesses. It was our task to identify the actual ingredients which produced the remarkable results that are discussed in motivational business books like *Firms of Endearment*.[1]

We've presented a practical guide and model for the way that business can be done. Much has been written on the subject of conscious capitalism or conscious business and although these publications are very good, we felt they were pitched at a philosophical level. We wanted to add to this important discussion by developing a methodology that would help in making the change happen at a very practical level. Although nobody is getting everything right, we've attempted to combine some best practices in a number of key areas that will guide organisations to transform and become more values-driven, purposeful, sustainable and profitable humanistic businesses.

The model defines the key areas that need to be consciously managed, in an integrated way, creating a purpose at its centre that at every investigation led to what we defined as 'stakeholder happiness'. It's an obvious truth that all human beings are seeking a state of happiness, although how people define happiness varies. The underlying drivers for self-improvement, community connection, positive social interaction with one another and authentic service to others, are what ultimately bring sustainable happiness to many. We found that many of these key areas were already familiar to any successful business, but it took great effort to identify the attributes that made a successful business humanistic or not.

The secret of what makes a humanistic business is embedded in the intention, attitude and overall sense of purpose that is ultimately baked into the DNA of the organisation. In each of the chapters that follow, we explain in more detail each section of the model, and why it matters.

As co-authors, we have each run successful businesses. We have managed significant multi-million dollar projects, and advised and coached companies operating in the billion-dollar realm. We came to realise that the success of each business and project was based upon people and relationships, and that these were the critical elements between success and failure. We recognised early on that a business can have the capability to succeed, and often had the strategy to achieve great things, and yet the psychological barriers and process-related inhibitors caused them and their projects to fail. We each became coaches in our lifelong journey to help leaders navigate through these challenges.

Using our personal experience, and working with small and large businesses, we discovered some common factors which made a difference for those organisations operating successfully in extremely challenging times. As a team, we operate from our Asia Pacific, US and European regions, which gives us a worldwide perspective on what is, and what is not, working in business internationally. We came together under a global brand as experienced business operators, as well as educators and coaches. This unique combination enables us to provide insights into what makes businesses work better and how to tackle the challenges that cause pain for owners and operators.

The benefits of being a conscious, humanistic business are now well researched, and the results are challenging organisations to start asking deeper questions about their purpose and how they can become more compassionate and service-oriented. Humanistic businesses are relationship-based, gain repeat business through referrals from loyal customers and, most importantly, create positive emotional connections between themselves and their clients. It's said that success is 80 per cent mind-set and 20 per cent mechanics, and we agree. It also starts with our thinking, which drives our behaviour, noting that good processes and systems also guide behaviour. Humanistic businesses simply think differently, they focus on different things, they find profit from the productive relationships they build and they connect with their own deeper purpose.

This is our collective contribution to the understanding of how a business achieves this intangible culture that has traditionally been difficult to identify and analyse. We propose a pull-type strategy to managing change, which attracts people to the change through inclusion and engagement. People and businesses will ultimately behave according to their values and current level of consciousness. However, we must change and business must become a force for good wherever it possibly can. We recognise that we are living in a different era of business and the skills and attitudes that were required for success in the old era are no longer relevant to the 21st century.

We are passionate about raising the consciousness of corporations and thereby the overall contribution of individuals and organisations. We therefore invite you to do good in the world, to connect, to love and engage with your higher purpose and leave a legacy that will continue to make a positive impact for generations to come.

[1.] Sisodia, R., Wolfe, D., Sheth, J. (2007). *Firms of Endearment: How World-Class Companies Profit from Passion and Purpose*, Pearson Prentice Hall.

Chapter 1

A New Era for Business

OVERVIEW
- Business is all about people, and positive and productive relationships.
- Business operates within lifecycles.
- Identifying and defining the seven key elements of a humanistic business.
- Gaining insights into the ultimate goal of operating a humanistic business.

Business is all about people and relationships. The combination of great people working under a loved brand name creates a synergy that is exciting to the marketplace. How a business and its team members engage, interact, communicate and influence people has a direct bearing on the potential for prospects to become clients, and clients to become long-term customers. People want to be engaged meaningfully, build relationships, be respected and to do and achieve things that make them feel great. They want to spend time with people who make them feel important and valued.

Business conducted through relationships of trust is a proven concept that goes back to when business first began. In today's fast-paced world, with limitless information, products and businesses to choose from, having the best product is no longer enough to assure success. Many inventors of the world's best products are broke, and most of those products are not the bestsellers in the marketplace.

Being the first to the market is not necessarily the answer either, as research and development absorbs money with no guarantee of a return on investment. True technology innovation now has a short market lifespan before it is no longer new, and many businesses are just waiting to copy it in order to enter the newly proven market early and capture it at a lower entry cost. They are, rightly or wrongly, interpreting R&D as Rip-off and Duplicate. Some say that is smart business. The truth is, products and services can be copied by any competitor in a very short time, and often at a lower cost. The differentiation must go beyond just the products and services to the unique brand distinction.

Although the quality and uniqueness of those products and services can contribute to the market value proposition, they are not the sole answer. The answer comes down to why consumers select one business or product over another. Sometimes it is location, stock availability, price or convenience, but they still prefer to transact with businesses that are friendly, consistent, predictable, stable and who can deliver on their promises. People simply want to do business with people they know, like and trust. While recognising that the success of a business is linked to their profile, their marketing and who is talking about them, the like and trust comes from a very personal connection.

We have identified seven core principles below that underpin the seven elements of the humanistic business model above; those of purpose, talent, values, vision, products, strategy and delivery. We believe that these principles are the key differentiators between businesses that are just doing well, and those that could be identified as humanistic businesses.

People prefer to do business with people who act with integrity.

Personal responsibility enables positive relationships.

People strive for repeatable positive experiences.

Enthused advocates energise market interest.

Strong positive brand energy attracts people.

Steady organic growth leads to sustainability.

Socially responsible interactions are good for business.

When these principles were recognised, applied, validated and confirmed, it became evident that the core aim of a business was to focus on team performance, using the humanistic business philosophy and approach. The highest-performing sustainable teams were somehow embedded with these principles, and living them. Those businesses had become humanistic through their teams.

People prefer to do business with people who act with integrity

Actions that represent integrity are demonstrated by an inner sense which enables people to like and trust others. The businesses that are loved add value, as they touch the human emotions in a way that makes people feel good. Those businesses are the ones people like to deal with, talk about, promote and recommend to others. These businesses recognise the importance of human relationships, of having fun and serving others as the only authentic way of doing business.

This is why operating as a humanistic business is critical during hard economic times, as well as sensible business practice during good times. Humanistic businesses attract loyal customers, service-focused suppliers and committed staff. This emotional connection to a business helps sustain it, allowing it to generate more referral business and greater profits, and this results in increased staff retention and a happier and more productive work environment. Neuroscience is now proving that the brain is all about connecting and cell communities, and this is a micro view of the society we live in. Even today's online technologies are about 'liking' people, joining groups and connecting.

In an increasingly interdependent world, networks are becoming an important way of connecting with others and doing business. The greater accessibility and transparency that goes with this means that those who contribute positively to the group get referred on, while those who don't often face potential exclusion. Exposure and accessibility have always been important in business, but the means for creating them have never been so numerous or fast. People have to be in the game to play it. Being the best at something is not good enough. One can be the best inventor or the most talented in a given field, but if no one knows about you, being the best becomes a wasted resource.

Human beings are highly suggestible and whether we like it or not, other people have a great influence on the way we think and behave. It's said that people are reflections of the books they read and the people they surround themselves with. Being surrounded by positive, enthusiastic people will inspire us, challenge us and support our growth, enriching our lives. The essence of an authentic relationship is one where all parties take responsibility for their actions and obligations and understand the impact upon those around them. Relationships are not a one-way commitment. This is reflected in the second principle of humanistic business:

Personal responsibility enables positive relationships

People directly influence the reputation and image of the business, whatever the circumstances of that interaction. Imagine the experience of being intentionally cut-up on the road by a truck and seeing the same driver abusing other road users. If that vehicle carries the brand name of a company, the view of that company will become tainted by the actions of that one individual. Team members need to live the ethos of the business they are involved with, as observers will assume they represent it.

These actions attract or repel others, and there does not seem to be much middle ground. The tone of voice, body language and the way people dress all have a significant influence on likeability. When it is desired to present a positive self-image, people need to take responsibility for those factors that support a positive interaction.

At the core of this personal responsibility is engaging with others, and building positive and sustainable relationships. This usually includes interacting with communities and contributing to wider society. Humanistic business is sometimes referred to as conscious capitalism, conscious business, socially responsible business or a social enterprise. Humanistic businesses can be highly profitable, yet profit is not their sole focus. They also focus on serving people and doing things better as a matter of conscious choice. It means reaching and stretching, learning and growing, becoming aware of personal goals and aspirations, of individual strengths and of the barriers that impede success.

Making a change to 'self' can be considered an inconvenience. It may be inconvenient to go out networking and meeting people instead of relaxing at home, or doing a good deed rather than focusing on oneself. Yet these actions of inconvenience allow a greater engagement with the world, more proactivity and the potential for greater benefit to all. Humanistic businesses are about using energy that shifts the norm, that drives through the inconvenience and results in positive change. The positive steps of one individual can have an influence on the many, with some pulled along in the wake of this energy.

Taking responsibility means recognising that personal experiences are the outcome of repetitive thinking and actions, and individuals have the ability to change that. When the shift from individual-thinking to group-thinking is made, this evolution above personal needs creates the potential for serving in the community for the greater good.

This philosophic approach raises awareness of the impacts that businesses can have at an emotional level on people and communities. When one runs a business with a genuine desire to serve others, they make people feel important. This has a direct influence on their wellbeing and, in return, they naturally want to reciprocate. It becomes an unselfish win-win outcome underpinned by authentic interactions.

People are the creators of their own feelings, but it is the interaction with their environment that their responses are based upon. There is a cause and effect relationship. Actions create experiences, and when those actions serve others, they become the cause of other people feeling good. This links to the third principle:

People strive for repeatable positive experiences

Operating as a humanistic business is easier with a strong understanding of the psychology behind human satisfaction. The more we know about people and their natural behavioural and communication styles, the more intimate engagement and interaction occurs. This makes the difference between a client feeling special, or having a sense of being just another customer. People know how it feels to be served by a smiling, friendly person, who seems genuinely concerned about their needs, as opposed to someone who appears disengaged and disinterested. It makes sense that the individual experience of that business is based on that personal interaction.

Every business that is loved triggers positive emotions, and generates excitement when dealing with them. More than just a financial transaction, it's bathed in feel-good emotions as a result of the actual experience, including the environment and other causal factors. When individuals enjoy an experience, the brain releases neurochemicals that create a good feeling. People delight in positive emotional states so much that they desire to repeat them. Emotions, and their impact on the ability to make product-buying decisions, are a distinctive human characteristic. People strive for good experiences and come to rely on them. Going back to a familiar business that consistently gives us a positive sense of being is something we tend to make a habit. Psychologists suggest that a habit takes 21 to 28 days to form. When applied to business, this tells us that any new process requires the staff to engage in a consistent and repetitive way for it to become a habit. It also means that a customer on the receiving end of a positive experience, such as excellent service each time contact is made with the business, will most likely return for more over the long term.

When a person has a great experience and then repeats that experience with the same business, their trust and confidence in the organisation's ability to provide a consistent quality experience naturally increases. Most of us prefer a predictable and reliable level of service. One of the benefits of great global franchises is that they offer an assurance of a similar experience regardless of where we travel in the world. They provide a sense of connection, of sameness. Positive experiences build on other positive experiences, firing up the same neural networks in the brain and thereby creating a stronger emotional bond each time. This builds customer loyalty and as a result, people have the confidence to promote the business or recommend it to others. If they have had multiple positive experiences and then one bad event, they are likely to disregard the negative event as an unusual or rare occurrence that would not likely change their overall view or on-going relationship.

When a team member, investor, observer or client becomes a positive advocate for the business, they start promoting it. Speaking highly about someone else's capabilities or business is a far more powerful marketing voice than self-promotion. When people are actively promoting the business and speaking about it, it is the brand energy at work, and this generates interest within the marketplace.

The greatest power of advocacy is positive promotion through the media. Television is particularly powerful as sound and video can conjure up more emotions than the print media or radio alone as it engages more of the brain. This means more potential to trigger our emotions. These days online videos that go viral can influence masses of people at low to no cost in very short periods of time. There are cases of people becoming overnight sensations and products being sold in large quantities due to their emotional connection to the viewers.

The most successful online marketing strategies tend to build a relationship over time where they are adding free value, and at the same time building likeability and credibility. Then comes the 'if you like this and want to learn more...' offer, and due to the trust created the customer clicks 'buy' and another sale is completed. People often see the end result and do not realise that it is the lead-up of the relationship to this sales point that is the key.

When people start referring others, and connecting and endorsing others online, they are offering a piece of their credibility to the business or product. When the online offer has reached a wide audience, it has the potential for high sales. Those who actively promote it become advocates – people who promote them in positive and active ways. When many people are promoting a particular person, product or business, it makes the potential sale a lot easier. People often become convinced through the advocate, reducing the need for direct sale effort. This is reflected in the fourth principle of humanistic business:

Enthused advocates energise market interest

The evidence that an organisation is operating as a humanistic business is best reflected in the existence of 'brand energy', which is the 'x-factor' that creates a culture of excitement, connection and collaboration. The underlying principles and best practices of becoming or operating as a humanistic business have largely been misunderstood. This is due to studies of these businesses being based on the results they enjoy from the brand energy that has been created, and not the specific factors that have created that energy. It's also difficult to compare the many micro causes that together create the energy that gives it momentum and power. To find the answers, it's necessary to look deep into the human psyche and have a greater understanding of how individuals interact with each other, and how emotional responses exist, as well as how they can be guided into a form of user experience.

Positive energy attracts positive energy, like attracts like, success attracts success. Our intent here is to look at the heart and soul of what constitutes a humanistic business which then creates and behaves consistent with those underpinning philosophies. Culture cannot be copied. Other businesses may mimic products but the best competitive edge is to build a unique culture that produces and sustains brand energy.

There are some brand names that attract a strong following of loyal customers who will forgive and overlook periodic product challenges. Some technology leaders have had high-profile technical issues during their product launches but due to customer loyalty, they were soon forgiven if not entirely forgotten. This provides a certain resilience, with the ability to survive bad experiences, and thrive despite them.

Global brands such as Apple, Harley Davidson, Porsche, Red Cross, eBay and Google offer a positive emotional reaction for those who engage with them. We are not identifying these as exemplars of humanistic businesses, but they (and others) are successful in adding value and creating a strong emotional significance for us. They become household names with enthusiastic fans who are loyal customers and effectively unpaid advocates for them. These fans wear the organisation's brand on their clothes, on their jewellery and even, in some extreme cases, have their logos tattooed on their bodies. It is this brand energy that makes the sight of their logo or the mention of their trade name trigger positive feelings within people. The brand has become an asset – it has a value. It has what accountants call goodwill, and what marketers call a presence. This is reflected in the fifth principle of humanistic business:

Strong positive brand energy attracts people

Whether we have had a personal positive experience, observed or heard great things about these organisations or recognised a brand as a household name independent of any conscious marketing efforts, we have witnessed the essence of brand energy. This is not an overnight process, a consequence of luck or just being in business long enough. It's far more than that. Just as some individuals exude radiance when they enter the room, brand energy can be likened to this charismatic energy effect. It's the result of our emotional response to the stimuli based on past personal experience, observation or the mystery that is created as people talk about the brand. At the deepest level of unconsciousness, it is the internal response, the feelings, the thoughts and the reactions to the external sensory inputs that make it happen. It influences the overall emotional state and sometimes the whole being and sense of inclusion.

Independent of any new product launch, there always seems to be a queue of people outside any Apple store waiting for the doors to open and the trading day to begin. The attraction that people have for the brand brings with it an air of excitement. The shop layout encourages collaboration, integrates people with technology and overwhelms the human senses with enthusiasm. Customers want to be inside the store, people want to be employed there, suppliers want to supply to them, investors want to hold shares in it, and it all comes down to the positive feeling that each of them experiences. Again, we're not suggesting that Apple scores highly in every area of our description of humanistic business, but it's a great example of where management of brand energy is done exceptionally well. This profile was originally down to one charismatic and visionary leader and the intensity with which he controlled the details of the experience. Whether Apple will maintain this market-leading vision and continue to reinvent and innovate after the loss of Steve Jobs, only time will tell. If his influence on the brand passes to the new generation of leaders and workers, it will be a testament to how brand energy can outlive its primary founders.

In law, a company is deemed the equivalent of a human person and can exist as an independent entity, owning its own assets and carrying its own debts. When a company depicts charismatic energy in its own right, and 'lives' as if it were a real person with its own values and belief systems, then it has a soul, and it truly lives. Disneyland became a reality and grew beyond even the imagination of its visionary founder, Walt Disney, and continues to be the largest attended theme park in the world. Why? Because it exudes brand energy.

People change, their needs and demands alter, the markets shift, and this is the key reason why innovation is crucial. Even Disneyland has reinvented itself many times over. Businesses need to go with the flow of the stream of change that represents the current of life and this new era for business.

The user experience that touches all key stakeholders is fundamental to the underlying philosophy of positive engagement. It explains why a person selects a particular coffee shop from a range of alternatives, or buys from one supplier over another. This human emotional response is what makes dealing with a particular business worthwhile. Whether it's the sense of self-importance, engagement, collaboration, connection or belonging, the cocktail of neurochemicals released that makes us feel alive, has real financial value to a business.

The term 'user experience' extends beyond the traditional focus on the client or customer and includes the wider interaction and engagement of staff, suppliers, investors, government and society. It explains why small local business owners who provide authentic customer care survive, despite competition from the larger chain stores who have greater buying power. It represents the fiscal value of this 'emotional economy', and it is the essence of customer loyalty which overrides the attachment to similar products and offerings of competitors. It represents the 'emotional quota' that becomes the differentiation strategy that is so hard to copy or replicate.

Over time, the brand gains power, and the goodwill associated with it makes the brand an asset. When people are talking about a business, it gives the brand more significance in the marketplace. This energy becomes the 'brand culture' and explains why only a Harley Davidson can feel like a Harley Davidson, independent of the likeness, functionality or look of its market alternatives. Some dedicated people will only buy a motorcycle when it carries the Harley Davidson insignia. The Harley Davidson insignia represents a way of life, and is not just a decorative piece of metal.

This relationship-based business approach is the reason why profitability can soar. The relationship extends beyond the organisation to its wider effects on society. Not only is employment helpful to society, but humanistic businesses, with their focus on doing the right thing, are conscious of their impact on the environment, the wider communities and other vulnerable groups such as animals.

While free-range eggs typically cost the consumer 20 per cent more than factory-farmed eggs, the consumer feels better within themselves that they are supporting an improved environment for the chicken. The cost of the business doing the right thing is effectively borne by the concerned consumer and, in most cases, higher profits can be enjoyed. The portion of revenue that is based on repeat business is a great way to measure success. If the organisation is an aid-based, not-for-profit concern or a government agency, then this revenue measure can be reflected in the funding it attracts on an on-going basis. The merit of measuring results based on repeat business is that it means customers are already coming back and this is likely as a result of their positive experiences.

This repeat business reflects loyal customers, and they help stabilise a business. In fact, humanistic businesses are generally not about fast growth usually achieved through acquisition or merger. Rather, humanistic businesses tend to grow steadily and organically. This facilitates the difficult process of embedding change into the culture, which takes time to do well. This growth then builds upon a solid foundation that is expanded and then stabilised, and built upon again. This is reflected in the sixth principle of humanistic business:

Steady organic growth leads to sustainability

The decision to become a humanistic business should be guided by the fact that doing the right thing by people, animals and the environment is morally justified, and feels right.

Building on solid foundations means that greater heights can be reached, but too many businesses try to build too fast without letting the concrete foundation cure. Organic growth is not unplanned, rather it is a clear strategy, implemented over time, with the intent of embedding change stage by stage, strategically and with the support and heart of the team.

This effectively allows innovation and stabilisation. In fact, it is a cyclic nature that is similar to all life forms. Apple started as a computer company, but after its peak, instead of ageing and dying, it reinvented itself into a music company, and at the end of the new cycle's peak, into a phone company. This innovation, or reinvention, is the breath of new life. What will be its next child?

Sustainability within is linked to a focus on sustainability externally. A commitment to greener practices that protect and nurture the earth, or a focus on contributing to the wellbeing of staff and their families, through to how a business interacts with the community all make for more sustainable relationships and living.

Put simply, doing good is good for business. This is reflected in the seventh principle of humanistic business:

Socially responsible interactions are good for business

Doing good makes people feel more comfortable, more positive about their actions, more confident about their contribution and having a greater sense of being respectful and being respected. Team members feel proud of their organisations and society becomes more accepting.

Take, for example, the community-building initiatives of the large mining companies. Even though they may have differing interests in many cases, and are sometimes driven by a focus solely on profit, they have learnt that contributing to the community helps make things happen. Imagine the benefits of doing the same activities for the right reasons. The rewards go beyond getting the job done, and include a sense of personal satisfaction and achievement that is consistent with the values of the person you truly are.

What some organisations have not realised is that it is more profitable to do the right thing. Building a business through productive relationships is not only more profitable, it is also more fun and far more sustainable than all other methods of doing business. The challenge is to be able to take a critical review of where businesses are today by honestly and truthfully recognising its current level of maturity.

A business that is focused on its relationships forces itself to keep up with the marketplace and its needs, as it is constantly tuned into, and listens intently to those it serves. This core value should aim to meet and ideally exceed those desires, thereby providing an exceptional user experience. This means not only providing exceptional experiences for all stakeholders, but having many mechanisms to capture their direct and indirect feedback in order to constantly innovate and improve. The main point is that feedback is not needed just to improve the state of the organisation. Feedback changes as markets change, and can be used as a feeder into innovation, so that business remains relevant to the marketplace. The better the relationship between business and customer the more is known about the customer's changing needs, and the better the business can meet those needs.

This is important as profit is directly linked to the level of service to others. Service considers all key stakeholders and not just the client, and also creates a positive emotional response in staff, suppliers, alliance partners, government and communities. We have found that the ultimate aim of a humanistic business is to achieve key stakeholder happiness.

KEY LESSONS

1. When you bring great people together, working under a loved brand name, the marketplace becomes interested in the synergy it creates.
2. The core aim of a humanistic business is to increase team performance, based on the humanistic business philosophy and approach.
3. There are seven core elements reflected in a humanistic business, comprising values, purpose, vision, talent, products, strategy and delivery.
4. The seven core humanistic business principles are:

   - people prefer to do business with people who act with integrity;
   - personal responsibility enables positive relationships;
   - people strive for repeatable positive experiences;
   - enthused advocates energise market interest;
   - strong positive brand energy attracts people;
   - steady organic growth leads to sustainability; and
   - socially responsible interactions are good for business.

5. Doing good has multi-faceted benefits that encompass the customer's sense of contribution and inclusion.
6. Profits are the outcome of doing good, even where costs go up.

Chapter 2

Aligning Personal and Business Values

OVERVIEW

- Shared personal and organisational values create the strongest bond for teams.
- Attracting team members with aligned values leads to greater staff retention.
- Acting authentically means you are operating in accordance with your values.
- Acting with consideration to natural universal cycles and laws allows an organisation to perform better.
- An environment that blends work and play encourages creativity and maximises innovation.
- The culture created by synergistic people is hard for competitors to replicate.

Having clarity about our personal and collective organisational values is the starting point for transforming any business into a humanistic business. The purpose and vision that defines the brand, and which ultimately creates the brand energy, comes from the alignment of personal and business values. The more humanistically centred the brand, the more powerful the brand energy. The values of an organisation are only demonstrable through the behaviours of its team members.

The strongest bond that synergises teams is that of shared values. Our values can be likened to a branch of a tree, and our beliefs are like the leaves on that branch. When our values shift, all our related beliefs are changed. Any dramatic circumstance that shakes up a person's life can lead to a shifting of that individual's values and have a significant and cascading impact on their life and business. Near-death experiences, the loss of a loved one, hearing traumatic news about one's family or exposure to extreme violence, are all examples of events that can reshape our values. The important point is that our values influence our thinking, and therefore behaviour and actions. They act as a filter and can either be the trigger for action or stop them altogether.

At its very heart, humanistic business is about authenticity and integrity, and these attributes are almost impossible to fake. At the same time, this area is where the potential for real differentiation and performance lies, both for individuals and organisations.

Individuals demonstrate authenticity when their actions have a clear alignment with what matters – which is alignment with their values. The amazing film-maker J. J. Abrams described his approach to film-making as a process from the inside out. He starts with a clear idea of his characters and then tenaciously stays faithful to this ideal as he tells the story. He says that if he were instead driven by the expectations of his audience, it just wouldn't work as the finished product would then lack true depth and substance.

Authenticity is the foundation stone of humanistic business. It provides clarity on who an individual is, where that individual adds most value, and is expressed through all aspects of the way they influence and engage with the organisation. It creates a sense of self-satisfaction, fulfilment, personal achievement and happiness. Life just feels like it works and their actions are congruent with their sense of being.

In any organisation, the collection of individual values, expressed through team behaviour, forms the culture of that organisation. When a business expresses a clear and unique sense of identity, the customer picks up on that. This is the brand energy in practice. Other businesses may be able to replicate a methodology, even a product, but it is very difficult to replicate the culture.

It is this process of working from the inside out; the creation of an internal reference point which becomes the springboard for everything else that follows. This self-knowledge gives rise to skilled decision-making and creative problem-solving and allows the development of strategies that are entirely consistent with the organisational purpose.

In fact, values are the foundation to everything that drives top performance. When strategy is based on values, they guide positive behaviours and actions towards their natural purpose. This means that until values align with true purpose, there is no single convergent point that enables total focus. When a business achieves clarity about its absolute direction, everything it does is aligned to serving that purpose.

Simon Bowen, international marketing manager at Rosscrae International, speaks about connecting with the business's 'nobility', which is the state or quality of being morally and spiritually good. He talks about finding the noble cause, that fundamental contribution which drives the organisation's vision and purpose. This also carries over to the worthiness of the work of the individuals and the team's collective nobility in working synergistically together for something greater than themselves and to which they can make a meaningful difference.

Values provide a fixed reference point from which to navigate the good and turbulent times. It's about living true to that inner guidance which represents who the organisation is and what they stand for, independent of the many external influencing forces. Values represent what is important to an individual as a whole and should guide every action and response. True values of an organisation do not change, whatever the environment, situation, person or circumstance. In fact, when values are totally embedded within it, the organisation retains its core values even in the event of a change of chief executive officer.

By aligning values, strategies and actions with purpose, individuals operate with integrity. Integrity is defined as the adherence to a code, but also as something that is in a state of being complete and undivided. So integrity is about consistency and wholeness. For a humanistic business, this wholeness refers to two things:

- **Intention** – this means having the positive intention and ability to satisfy a number of potentially conflicting values simultaneously. Individuals often unconsciously satisfy a single dominant need based on a specific situation, so they may act at the expense of other important factors. For example, a person may recognise that health is an important value but if achievement is regarded as a more powerful value, that individual may behave in ways that will satisfy achievement, but at the expense of their health. A humanistic business will stay true to its intention towards its purpose and genuinely attempt to balance all these important values. This means managing people, planet and purpose with the same priority as profit. Arguably, by focusing on doing the right thing and serving others, profit becomes the reward and an indicator of getting it all right.

- **Inclusion** – this means embracing stakeholder inclusivity in a meaningful way, including all those groups that have a direct and indirect impact on your organisation's performance, such as investors, employees, partners (suppliers), customers and society. A humanistic business will consider the influences of each of these groups on the whole organisation.

Bringing all this together by aligning individual, team and organisational values, strategies, actions and purpose, where individuals act with integrity that is guided by intention and inclusion, is what creates the focal point of humanistic convergence. This is the key aim of the humanistic business, or at least to act in a way that seeks to achieve it.

In practice, a business has to look deep within itself to find its true purpose. People with shared values create the right environment to act with integrity. It also means bringing the right people together to use their natural skills in meaningful ways, working in teams that respect and share the same intention to serve for the benefit of others. The trick is to recognise the collective benefits rather than adopt a 'what's in it for me?' position.

This is not an easy alignment, but when it becomes the norm to act in ways that support this approach, the essence of a humanistic business is achieved. If a company's focus on profitability becomes the single dominating driver for all behaviour, then it may be at the expense of other important company interests such as sustainability, employee happiness or community relations. Profit is the outcome of working within a framework that leads to humanistic convergence, but it's not the sole driver. It's smart to consider it a measureable indicator of doing good in business, and use it as a check that customers are being engaged.

Money enables growth and expansion. The lack of it can cause an organisation to go out of business, or the timeliness of the cash flow will have an enormous impact on its sustainability. If serving is a core part of humanistic business, then money and a managed cash flow is essential in order to continue that service. In this sense, money needs to be respected for its ability to assist an organisation to expand and sustain itself. But the love of money, when it becomes a driver for greed and power, is the negative side, and humanistic businesses avoid that by maintaining a focus on its purpose and service, and not solely on personal gains.

Enabling Growth

Often complexity is used as an excuse for lack of creativity in growth or committing to real change, both by individuals and organisations. It's possible to end up getting caught up in the continued pursuit of a myriad of external goals while neglecting the truths related to the core purpose.

Humanistic business looks towards natural universal cycles and laws, and how they can be applied to business. Consider a basic element of life like water. Water is an essential requirement for life. Stagnant water is unhealthy, causes disease and can poison us and the environment. Flowing water, on the other hand, has energy, and so its life-saving essence is preserved. The observation of this natural flow shows that life is about movement. We know that lack of movement in the body leads to atrophy. Even the brain's neural networks, when not being used, start to breakdown and undergo a process known as pruning. All this tells us that movement is essential to life, and it's also critical to business.

A business that is not changing or evolving, is stagnant, and risks ageing and dying. This means that reinvention, evolution and sustainability, coupled with a desire to take performance to the next stage of growth, gives life to business. Individuals with growing self-awareness and clarity of intent tend towards an evolution of consciousness that moves beyond survival thinking and towards self-actualisation. It is the process by which people move towards achieving their full potential and realising 'flow'. This journey moves through the satisfaction of fundamental personal needs and develops into an interest in service beyond the confines of self-interests. Humanistic business therefore aims, at the final result of its journey, to fully evolve to a level of consciousness that not only satisfies the survival needs of the group, but also expresses its full potential at all levels.

Clearly, the financial survival of an organisation is of paramount importance but as the consciousness of any organism matures, then the systems, processes and means of survival become part of its way of doing business. Conscious integration leads to the successful management of all the contributing factors that makes the organisation achieve its outcomes, by focusing on strategy, systems, processes and behaviours.

As the 'people' elements are the most critical, all the strategies, systems and processes, while important, must be focused on enabling the people and relationships to flourish. When people are guided by solid values, clear strategies and a strong purpose, and supported by helpful technologies, systems and processes, they are able to act with integrity.

Identify, Clarify and Satisfy Values

The important process to understand is the enablement and alignment of individual and organisational values. Many organisations have declared values, but values are only demonstrable through behaviour and actions. It is a common occurrence to witness individuals and organisations claiming certain values, only to find behaviour to be entirely inconsistent with that claim. A business must walk its talk to build its trust in the marketplace.

As Antony Jenkins, CEO of Barclays bank, explained after taking over the top job at the crisis-hit organisation:

> 'We need to change our culture, which means setting out the values you expect from people and deal with those that don't follow them . . . We will be judged by our behaviour, not what we say . . .'[1]

Clarifying values is often harder than we think. The initial temptation is simply to intellectualise the process and identify those things that are perhaps socially acceptable and therefore what others want to hear. People brainstorm a set of values that makes them feel good at the time, but which they may not be able to demonstrate or be willing to adhere to later.

Take health, for example. Our culture tells us that health is an important commodity and our language is rich in expressions like, 'without your health . . . what have you got?' Most people, when they start to identify their values, will put health somewhere near the top of their list. However, when they examine their behaviour, many find that health is so far down their list it never gets managed. When faced with situations where we have limited resources, as many of us do on a daily basis, those things that are most important will always take priority. We know health is important, but when it comes down to it, we've got to get to work, look after the kids and manage the rest of our life, so looking after our own health never gets high enough up the priority list.

Similarly, if you're the CEO of a company, you are aware that integrity and ethics is important, but if you've got your investors breathing down your neck, you know you've got to achieve the financial results, whatever it takes. The emphasis goes to the 'no matter what it takes', and we may compromise our values to make it happen. A lot of individuals and organisations find themselves in this position. When faced with limited resources and conflicting priorities and reality bites, you do whatever it takes to do the things you value the most or that have become the most important to achieve.

In terms of identifying values, start by being brutally honest about where you are at today. This examination of consistent behaviours over time will tell you everything you need to know about your current value set. It then becomes a question of whether that behaviour is a true representation of you performing at your full potential. Values identification begins with listing the key areas of importance to you and their order of priority. When you do this in a group, the common values may start to become more obvious. To validate them is to then witness, analyse and compare your behaviour to the list as evidence of what you are doing as to what you perceive is important.

When personal awareness is increased, values become clarified and recalibrated. With a more enlightened consciousness, people have the clarity to challenge conditioned values and potentially create entirely new ones. Humanistic businesses are not afraid to challenge industry or cultural dogma and creatively and courageously express their uniqueness. Admittedly, it is possible to behave with authenticity and integrity and still perform badly. However, humanistic business outcomes are definitely not about mediocrity. Our observation is that those who are enlightened enough to build their code of behaviour around unique self-expression and integrity also set the performance bar very high for themselves and those they deal with. Excellence is inherent within a highly conscious humanistic business. That is why doing well and doing good can be two sides of the same coin.

Even meeting industry benchmarks is not the answer, as they are effectively an averaged measure of the industry norms. Humanistic businesses not only aim to excel beyond industry norms, they have the confidence to question, test and often change them. In some respects, they discard them as irrelevant and lead the industry in new directions. This is because industry norms can often be stagnant measures of the past. They assume the market is not changing, and that what worked in the past is the right way of acting. Yet technology and new innovations are changing so dramatically that yesterday's practices can fast become out of date. Within an industry where competitors are quick to copy the leaders, innovation must outpace the copycatting.

Clarifying Values

Experience and external influences often deepen our understanding of ourselves and clarify our values. We are currently living through times characterised by significant change, with huge shifts in social expectations, dramatic increases in the awareness of what we find acceptable and what we do not and some of the most challenging economic times in history. This is the new era of business we described earlier.

Perhaps understandably, many are frustrated with the behaviour of our leaders in the areas of business, politics and media, and activities that were perhaps tolerated before are no longer acceptable to us now. We have witnessed the unravelling of the financial services sector and the resulting light that has been shone into the innermost workings of the culture, which has brought most of the developed world to the brink of financial disaster. Most people don't like what this has revealed and questions have been asked about the very ethos that underpins our economic system.

This is not an exercise in pointing blame at any particular industry or sector, but most people don't like what they see and they want change. We can use these experiences as awareness-raising evidence and a reflection of where we are in our evolution of consciousness. Hopefully, these observations can provide a behavioural reference point for what we don't want to be repeated. But although these experiences may expose the problem, they don't necessarily provide solutions. Real change only comes from within, from a conscious decision to experience something differently, whether that be for an individual, an organisation or society. Real sustainable change first begins within the individual. This journey of authenticity is not only an alignment of personal and group values, but also an out-flow of a strength of individual identity and the legacy and impact that each person leaves on the world. Although humanistic business ultimately is not all about an individual it starts with each of us as individuals. It begins with individuals and progresses into teams, and then the power of its influence spreads to the organisation and, finally, is reflected in its cultural norms.

Those businesses that adapt and rise to the challenges in this new era will have the potential to thrive, and those that don't, will become extinct. For any organism to survive in a rapidly changing environment, adaptability is crucial. Based upon our research on the success of humanistically run businesses we believe in the near future, for a business to survive and sustain profitability, it will have to demonstrate at least some of the behaviours described and thereby develop the values associated with a humanistic business approach.

When individuals and organisations evolve beyond thinking solely about survival, they become more concerned with questions of meaning, purpose, impact and legacy. There's no paradox in this increased self-knowledge that gives rise to a greater concern for others. It's a characteristic of the conscious journey. There are certain behaviours that characterise humanistic businesses, as well as core reasons why more organisations are demonstrating these attributes.

The reactionary forces experienced in the world of politics and business are only part of the picture. There are social factors at play too, which are changing the bedrock of our culture. Many developed cultures with an ageing population have a greater influence on the values of that culture. In 2010, some 19 countries had a median age of over 40 years. These countries are led mainly by developed countries such as Japan, Germany and Italy.[2] In 1989, for the first time in its history, the majority of adults in the US were over 40 years old.[3] In most cases, many people are continuing to play an active contributory role by staying in work much longer than would have been the case in earlier times.

One significant factor of this trend is that as individuals mature they tend towards what Abraham Maslow describes as 'increased autonomy, and resistance to enculturation'. According to Maslow, members of this same group move away from purely security-based behaviour and towards a higher level of behaviours and interests such as esteem of self as well as of others, creativity and morality. All the attributes he included fall into the category of self-actualisation. In other words, the decision-makers of our society are increasingly made up of individuals who are less influenced by social trends and the expectations of others, and far more interested in personal fulfilment, but also in contributing to entities that exist outside themselves. They are often at a particular point in their life cycle where they are more financially secure and are increasingly interested in meaning, contribution and legacy. Some writers see this as not just a natural life-cycle factor for individuals, but as a general raising of consciousness within our species.

In the book *Firms of Endearment*, the authors describe the present era as the Age of Transcendence whereby physical (materialistic) influences give way to the metaphysical (experiential).[4] Also, in the book *A Whole New Mind*, author Daniel Pink describes a similar phenomenon as a shift from the Information Age into this Conceptual Age. His assertion is that companies who wish to take advantage of this new age should develop values away from the purely rational, left-brain perspective and towards the more subjective, emotional, creative perspectives most often associated with the right side of the brain.[5] It's important to note that this is not about reducing profit, rather the opposite. Increased profit is attainable through building relationships that lead to repeat business and referrals.

Creating Value by Aligning with all Stakeholders' Values

We've already explained that humanistic businesses tend to demonstrate integrity in their actions by consciously managing all of the stakeholder relationships. Humanistic businesses recognise the value of aiming to satisfy the interests and values of all of the groups who affect the performance of the company. This may mean that their relationships with employees, including unions, suppliers, the communities in which they operate, as well as investors, are all infused with a genuine desire to understand and satisfy values on both sides. Such businesses are often viewed more as partnership arrangements which recognise their interdependent nature. In some cases, this is built into the framework of the corporate structure, perhaps in the form of genuine employee partnerships, share ownership or other profit-sharing schemes. Often the unions are included in a transparent management process and are party to, and also contribute towards decision-making.

Suppliers are often seen as 'inside the fence' and their profitability, efficiency and longevity is managed with the same priority as traditional 'internal' relationships. These partnerships must not be confused with cosy, sloppy arrangements that do not benefit from the pressures of normal market forces. The commercial terms should still be highly competitive, but with the benefit of greater transparency, improved communication and problem-solving through increased mutual understanding and commitment.

This integration with stakeholders has some interesting consequences. Often the method for reaching agreement between parties is through traditional negotiation. However, closer partnering coupled with clarity of values allows all parties to be more creative about how those values and interests are satisfied. Rather than seeing a fixed pie of resources whereby 'more for me means less for you', the building of trust and transparency between partners means that solutions can be much more fluid and flexible, as long as the fundamental interests of each party are being satisfied.

Taking the Longer-term Perspective

One of the behavioural traits associated with increased awareness is the ability to resist short-term pressures and take a more long-term view. Just as enlightened parents see beyond the immediate demands of their children to nurture responsible, self-sufficient and independent adults, humanistic businesses seem to be able to steer a course through short-term demands to remain driven by the bigger and fuller picture. This can be extremely difficult if success is measured by re-election to office or even the next quarterly results, and it may be that a new measure for success is required. Again, without a clear view of values, it's easy to be distracted by external reference points and expectations.

This dichotomy was illustrated by a piece of research done in the area of health. In October 2007, a UK government-funded group called *Foresight* published the results of a study on obesity.[6] It was conducted by nearly 250 scientists over a two-year period and their brief was to 'examine the causes of obesity and map future trends to help the government plan effective policies both now and in the future.' The findings were multi-factorial, but there were some key underlying factors that underpinned behaviour and which are interesting with regard to our reference point for success. The study observed that the environment in which human beings evolved and the environment where we now find ourselves now are almost polar opposites. Early man's experience was that food was relatively scarce and they had to work hard to get it. The shift in the effort to hunt food to the processed means of today's food supply has led to a more common obesity problem in modern life.

This polarity means that the environment we have created for ourselves is working against our most fundamental design. However, it is now so much a part of the fabric of modern behaviour, we stop noticing it. The research reported that we are 'sleepwalking' towards an epidemic and they were surprised that there were some 'outliers' in this environment which resisted the powerful cultural forces at play and behaved differently. As a result, they got different outcomes. Our point here is about where you place your reference point – within or without yourself or your industry. There's an enormous difference between what is natural (your internal reference) and what is normal (external reference). Just because your conditioning and your culture tell you this is the way to behave, whether it is to do with food, business, relationships or health, doesn't mean that it actually works for you. So how do you measure success? The influence of our conditioning and culture are undeniable; this is simply about raising awareness, enabling us to make a difference and live by conscious choices that are more closely aligned with our personal values.

These things are played out with other powerful energies in our lives. If we examine our relationship with food, for example, we realise that we make sound eating decisions based on a number of key factors – does it look good, taste good, smell good? What does our family food history tell us about how we eat, where we eat and how much we eat? However, if we start to broaden our awareness of the digestion of food and other physiological factors we start to ask other questions, such as 'how do I feel after eating my food, how well is my body digesting or eliminating, and how slow must I eat to catch up with the body's sensory indicators that I am full?' This is one of the definitions of integrity in that having a complete awareness and understanding of the impact of your decisions and behaviour in all areas is important. It's not that some of the earlier questions about taste, smell and look are unimportant. Clearly they are, it's just that they are incomplete. Once we've broadened our awareness to reflect more fully on the entire experience of eating, we ask different questions of the outputs and perhaps start to make different decisions about the inputs.

There is increasing validity in measuring performance over longer periods that perhaps extend beyond the current tenure and will only benefit the next generation. There is often a big difference in the quality of decision-making if it's done to satisfy the interests of the current incumbent compared to making decisions that acknowledge the life and performance of the organisation beyond any personal interests. As a result of these forces, humanistic businesses often favour an organic growth model over a merger or acquisition in terms of growth. Although this may result in a slower growth process, it's more likely to manage and maintain alignment with their existing values and thereby retain the built-in integrity and authenticity. Through merger or acquisition, there is the risk of diluting this alignment if an entirely different value set and therefore culture is being integrated into the organisation. The forces at play may counter one another.

Creating a Culture of Creativity and Innovation

Another trait of humanistic businesses is the ability to create an environment which successfully blends work and play. This integration creates a workspace that engenders creativity and innovation. Creating environments like this allows us to strike at the heart of what it means to be a fully actualised human being, and thereby encourages optimum personal performance. At its most fundamental level, our sense of engagement with, and full participation in, life is what we strive for. Our earlier definition of authenticity is to be real, and sometimes that human drive to be alive overrides personal risk.

In contrast, our life today is characterised by the management of risk. This, of course, at some level is an expression of the understanding of the value of life, but at the same time, the mitigation of risk in every conceivable area insulates us from the very force we are trying to protect. We have huge fluffy pillows between ourselves and the vitality of life, and our experiences of its immediacy become dulled and remote. The sense of control shifts from within to without.

Today, the legislators and rule-makers in our society, well intentioned as they may be, aim to protect us from the vagaries of modern life and define how we should behave. If we are no longer the responsible actor in our life, then we become a remote spectator. There has been some interesting research done in areas related to this phenomenon. One of the highly structured and regulated areas of life in developed countries is the road traffic system. Despite the multitude of signs, road-markings and explicit threats like traffic cameras, some traffic junctions continue to be problematic. There is now a traffic management system that is growing in popularity around the world which takes the opposite approach to managing risk, and which is demonstrating spectacular results. It was conceived in Holland where they call it 'woonerf'. In these 'roads' the pedestrians, cyclists and motorists get more or less equal share of the same space and the Dutch government has reported a drop in accident rates of 40 per cent within these zones. The concept is that there is very little formal signage and there are no kerbs as the pavement blends with the road. It is difficult to discern who has right of way or priority, particularly at junctions. This means that those entering the zone have to proceed with significantly heightened awareness and at lower speed.

Paul Watters, head of transport policy at the UK Automobile Association, says: 'Woonerfs work by changing the psychology. Is it a road or is it a path?'[7] The very absence of instruction forces users to be more responsible that in some ways seems totally counter-intuitive. One of the consequences of much greater personal awareness is greater personal responsibility. However, this sense of personal responsibility means you are in the game rather than observing from the side lines.

Alignment between Individual and Organisational Values

Our observation and research has shown that in those organisations where personal and group values are most aligned, effectiveness, integration and performance are at their optimum. External forces are a factor but, as with individuals, transformation is most powerful when driven by internal motivators. The powerful changes in our cultural environment enable us to raise awareness and perhaps challenge our dominating perspectives, but real change only occurs by clarifying values and then aligning them with core behaviour. The current external pressures in our society are therefore helpful in changing our perspective.

Real change will only come about by leaders at every level in the organisation recalibrating the culture that pervades every activity. This is not about just realigning visions and mission statements, although that will be part of the wider change process, it is about a fundamental change in the prevailing behaviour so it aligns with our values. Part of the challenge of this process is that the current leaders often thrived in the old order. But the move towards authenticity eventually becomes the main strength of an organisation that develops in this way. By defining, guiding and developing culture through behaviour and clear leadership, it will provide a uniqueness that is difficult to replicate.

Even if a competitor sets out to model and copy your systems and methodology, the result will be entirely different because success is built upon values, behaviour and cultural integrity rather than procedures and mechanical methods. A humanistic business approach brings the people and life to otherwise stagnating policies, procedures, information systems and processes.

KEY LESSONS

1. Brand energy is the demonstration of organisational values and gives the company a non-replicable competitive edge in the market.
2. Values are the foundation to everything that drives us.
3. When our values, strategies and actions towards our purpose are aligned, we are operating with integrity.
4. Corporate purpose is defined by values and must be strong enough to attract and align everything and everyone to that purpose.
5. A business that is not evolving and changing is stagnating and dying.
6. When organisations evolve beyond survival thinking, they become concerned with questions of meaning, purpose, impact and legacy.
7. When alignment of values is created between all stakeholders, profits soar.
8. Identifying the executive team's core values is the starting point for determining organisational values.

1. http://www.theguardian.com/business/2013/feb/13/barclays-antony-jenkins-reputation

2. www.parliament.uk/briefing-papers/sn03228.pdf, page 6

3. Sisodia, R., Wolfe, D., Sheth, J. (2007). *Firms of Endearment: How World-Class Companies Profit from Passion and Purpose*, Pearson Prentice Hall.

4. Ibid.

5. Pink, D. (2006) A Whole New Mind: Why Right-Brainers Will Rule the Future, Riverhead Trade.

6. http://www.bis.gov.uk/foresight/our-work/projects/published-projects/tackling-obesities/reports-and-publications

7. http://www.telegraph.co.uk/motoring/road-safety/9086705/Why-woonerfs-will-change-how-we-drive.html

Creating Dynamic Teams

Organisations thrive when the right people are in the right roles. Businesses generally employ team members based on their talent, and replace them if their values don't align with those of the business. Values alignment is the most critical factor in selecting team members, as an individual's personal values are the best indicators of having passion and longevity for the role. Unfortunately, identifying personal values is the hardest part of the recruiting process.

Not-for-profit organisations often attract eager and loyal team members, as the prospects want to work for *that* organisation because of the work it is doing, and how it aligns with their own personal values and sense of doing something of importance.

When it comes to nurturing personal talent, skills and expertise, it's best to look at a prospect's natural behavioural style as the best indication of their capabilities and potential. Where the role offered is suited to the individual's personal behavioural strengths, and their values align with those of the organisation, you have the ingredients for a brilliant new recruit. The importance of having staff in roles where they demonstrate their natural talents has an enormous impact on the overall performance of any team. In fact, our research found that building a humanistic business is largely about concentrating on team performance. By profiling individuals and teams, an understanding of the personality composite of teams and the inherent strengths and weakness of each team member can be discovered and utilised. This allows the identification of the teams' weak points, what additional resources are required and whether the individual team members are in the right job for their innate strengths. Team members are looking for two key things in their leaders: clarity and a sense of importance. Clarity comes in the form of knowing what their role is and what authority they have, where the organisation is going and what it is trying to achieve, what their specific tasks are, how they personally fit into the profile of the team, what value they can offer and what they will be held accountable for.

Helping them to feel important is vital in any humanistic business, as this means the team members feel they are listened to, they have a stake in the business, they feel respected and have a sense of pride in what they do and what the business does. When people feel valued they want to perform and they will be committed to working towards the team's goals.

Educational psychologist Dr Bruce Tuckman recognised that teams develop within a defined cycle of Forming, Storming, Norming and Performing as well as adjourning when the team is disbanded.[1] The study of this natural cycle shows that to get to 'norming', the team must be clear about the direction of the organisation or team, and their personal and team strengths and skills. The military are strong on the discipline of adhering to ranks in terms of not being able to question the authority of the leader, and this is critically important on the battlefield as it maintains the team in 'norming'. When there is a change in, or loss of, a team member, they go back to 'forming', but a strong culture and clarity of roles and responsibilities can bring them up to 'norming' in a short amount of time. Going back to the military example, if the leader is lost on the battlefield, the disciplined training automatically places the next highest ranked officer in charge – no questions asked. This is necessary because of the risks associated with the loss of a leader in the highly emotional and adrenaline-based environment of war.

Studying the state of norming, and the need for attaining that state to get to the 'performing' phase, the answer is to focus on clarity. This is achieved through many tools that help to identify expertise, define roles and responsibilities and guide behaviours. These include CVs, behavioural profiles matrixes, organisational charts, job titles, job descriptions, organisational and project plans, policies, terms of reference documents, contracts and defined rules of engagement.

Of these, the behavioural profile is the best predictor of a person's potential and how they are likely to act in stressful situations. An added benefit of behavioural profiling is that once each team member has a better understanding of themselves and their fellow team members, a natural beneficial culture begins to emerge organically. People stop drawing conclusions about another person based upon their own prejudices and begin to understand their differences with more empathy so that acceptance can grow. As a result, team cohesion is achieved.

The quality of the people is the chief factor in determining the capabilities of an organisation. Great businesses attract, hire and retain exceptional people. It's these people who create, influence and maintain its culture. They either make or break the business, and decisions on their selection, development and the roles they play must be taken with care.

The principle of recruitment is to identify key people whose talents meet the needs of the business and whose values are aligned with it. Individuals may be highly competent but if their values, beliefs and attitudes don't sit comfortably with the ethos of the business, this can inhibit the organisation's overall performance. A progressive organisation employs people who can contribute to the culture in a positive way.

To understand the complexity of people dynamics it's necessary to understand how personal competencies, behavioural style, communication style and values contribute to the overall success of the team. These integrated elements are what make human beings complex and difficult to predict.

Developing Natural Talents

Every person has a unique core behavioural style that represents their natural talents. Individual natural talents enable people to do certain things more easily and more efficiently than others, and using these natural skills allows individuals to expend less energy in certain tasks. Often people may not even be aware of these gifts as they do specific tasks with so much ease that they don't even consider that others might find them difficult. Think of your individual strengths and the tasks where people most often ask for your help, you may gradually become aware of what those gifts are. Interestingly, people can see the gifts more easily in others because they recognise the difference between another's abilities and their own.

People's natural talents represent their potential for excellence. They are part of an individual's growth potential and if developed, can become key strengths. Ultimately, when they are developed into high competency skills, the state of flow is achieved. Flow is the state where life seems easier, enjoyment fuller with achievement happening in the shortest amount of time. In his 2008 bestseller *Outliers*,[2] author Malcolm Gladwell proposed his '10,000-hour rule' which is the likely number of hours of guided practice it takes to get people from growth to flow. The state of flow is not a natural state – it is a developed state that builds on natural strengths reflected in individual core behavioural styles. Behavioural profiling ends up being the fastest and easiest way to recognise individuals' growth potential.

The opposite of flow is ebb. If flow can be likened to swimming down the stream with the current, ebb would be trying to swim upstream against the current. Ebb takes more energy, and is more exhausting. Unfortunately, a lot of people have pushed through the barriers and developed proficiency in areas for which they have no passion – they are good at their job, but have no love for it. Their job will absorb more of their energy than they realise, and their lack of passion makes the role less enjoyable. These two states are shown graphically by considering the interplay of competency and passion.

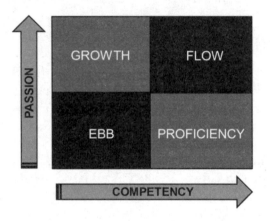

To explain how this works is to understand the operation of the brain. The human brain has billions of neurons and when they connect to each other through what are known as synapses, neural networks are formed as communication pathways. Every thought triggers or re-fires a neural network, and the more people have that same thought, the stronger the association. The neural network's strength becomes based upon repeated dominant thinking patterns.

When people begin learning a new skill new neural network begins firing using the conscious brain. This is known as unconscious incompetence, meaning that the conscious mind has to be doing all the work and is a high concentration state when learning something new. As the neural networks in the brain are firing in new ways, it creates a web of synaptic relationships. Imagine the first time sitting behind the steering wheel of a car without knowing how to operate the controls. Imagine receiving instructions and consciously trying to interpret the overload of new information, taking pieces of data into an order, which then becomes a knowledge base information (structured data). The more experience each person gains results in repeated firings of these neural networks, as each person in the learning process moves to the state known as 'conscious incompetence' where the conscious mind is trying to make sense of the information.

As individuals continue to repeat a task, and start applying the information and giving it meaning, it becomes knowledge. Knowledge is the outcome of applied information. When that meaning becomes consistent and the results are repeated we condition the mind to repeat those results with a less conscious focus, we reach a conscious competence level. Over time, we become capable of repeating it using less brain power, energy and concerted focus.

As the patterns of behaviour keep repeating the activity, the neural network keeps firing and becomes an even stronger communication pathway until a state of 'unconscious competence' is reached. Once the state of unconscious competence is reached the behaviour or activity can be accomplished with little conscious thought and the subconscious mind starts taking control of the process naturally and automatically in an integrated manner, providing higher performance and competency. This explains how repeated experiences improve performance, by impacting both the conscious and the unconscious mind. Persistence in repeated tasks ultimately leads to becoming an expert in that field, although arguably perfect practice makes for a perfect skill. So if a person is repeating a flawed process, then that process will effectively be embedded in their brain. Research has shown that injury-prone people are likely to be that way as a result of a flawed thinking strategy or pattern. If they are using the same thinking patterns that led to that behaviour, they will of course get similar results and remain prone to injury.

This four-stage competence model was initially developed by the Gordon Training International organisation in the 1970s, being attributed to an employee named Noel Burch.[3] While the development of neural networks is evident, the challenge is that the brain also reduces the networks that are not being used over time. This natural phenomenon is known as pruning. This explains why a skill that isn't used in many years results in a reduction in competency. However, an individual can develop the competency again far faster than when first learnt because the neural network still exists, albeit with less complexity and strength.

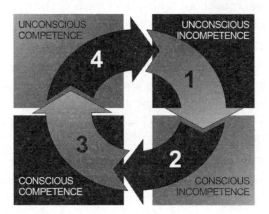

In summary, competency leads to expertise, and expertise enables value, which in turn links to contribution. The trick is to support teams by identifying their natural talents, helping develop them on their path to achieving flow as well as access to the relevant education, coaching and resources and giving them the right role in which that flow can be leveraged for the business. In their flow state staff will already be passionate about the business's values and objectives, so in looking at how to bring out their flow to the benefit of the business, an organisation is additionally supporting their own innermost desires.

Behavioural Style

A humanistic business strives to get each team member to tap into their natural talents, to develop and refine their flow and then bring that into the team's collective expertise where synergy makes the whole team flow. Before we can fully appreciate team synergy, we must look more into the behavioural attributes of the individuals. We are all born with a specific behavioural style and while we may adapt that style to suit different environments, we don't completely change it.

Building on our natural gifts means aligning our professional development with our natural behavioural style. When we have reached a high level of competence we are able to get into that state of flow where we do exceptional work, using our energy wisely, and we enjoy what we are doing. But this concept of flow is not new. The ancient Chinese oracle, the I-Ching (Book of Changes), which is more than 3,000 years old, is based on this concept of flow.

The yin–yang philosophy demonstrates that there are two seemingly opposing but interconnecting forces at play in every living thing. From a human perspective, these can be likened to strengths and weaknesses. The I-Ching recognises that when two elements are divided into four, more clarity results as the detail in each increases, then even more when four elements are divided into eight, and eight into 16, etc. The I-Ching explains that in all these complexities there is also simplicity as the elements are broken down into finer distinctions. This is the fundamental principle of how having a more complex and developed neural network enables an individual to do things more simply and easily.

The Greek historian Hippocrates (460-370 BC) defined four ancient temperaments that suggested there were four key behavioural differences. He linked behaviours back to body fluids, known as humours. One of the most studied and popular models is the DISC behavioural system, which presents a four-quadrant behavioural model based on the work of the late psychologist Dr William Moulton Marston.[4] In aligning these models, yellow bile represents the 'D' or powerful choleric personality; blood represents the 'I' or popular sanguine personality (the optimist); phlegm represents the 'S' or the peaceful phlegmatic personality; and black bile represents the 'C' or the perfect melancholy personality.

DISC is an acronym for: *Dominance* or *Driver*, which relates to driven, control, power and assertiveness styles; *Influence*, which relates to highly social and communication styles; *Steadiness* (*Submission* in Dr Marston's time), which relates to patience, persistence, stable, thoughtfulness and security-focused styles; and *Compliance*, which relates to structure, detail and organisation-based styles.

It's important to understand that of these four attributes, a person may be dominantly one of them, two of them, or have a blend of up to three of the behavioural strengths, but cannot be strong in all of them. This appears to support the theory that human beings work most effectively in teams. People can be assessed against the DISC model based on the findings that D and C styles were more task-oriented, and I and S styles more people-oriented. Dr Marston also found that D and I styles were more active, which Dr Carl Jung called extrovert, with the I trait being most extroverted of the styles. He found C and S styles were more passive, which Dr Carl Jung called introverted, with the C trait being most introverted.

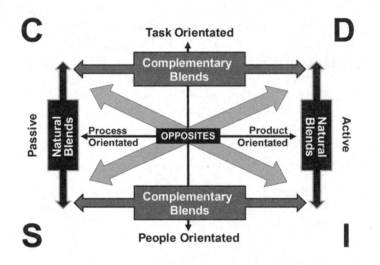

People with traits opposite to ours usually cause us the most challenges as they think differently and want different things. Yet each person needs those opposites to protect themselves from overdoing their strengths. Interestingly, people with similar behavioural styles tend to have closely aligned views on common sense, whereas those with opposite styles have a very different perspective. This means there is no universal common sense. Task-oriented people see common sense as based on logical actions, while those with people-oriented traits approach it from a 'people' perspective. When we recognise these styles, their complexities and how they integrate with each other, we have a greater respect for the team, a better understanding of how each style brings its own strengths and value to the team and so are better equipped to lead a high-performing team.

There are many behavioural-based profiling tools. Some of them use acronyms, some use colours and some even refer to animal names or categories to explain the differences, but all use the same biological references for the human body. It's believed that the core behaviour relates to the speed and temperature of the blood flowing through the brain. The only time the core behaviour changes is under extreme stress, and during these times the blood vessels constrict, changing the pressure of the blood flow and thereby altering the speed and temperature of the blood. This reveals that personal wellbeing is critical to being able to function at an optimum level.

Team Dynamics

Following the Chinese process of applying the division principle to distinguish finer detail, the study of the I-Ching suggests an eight core behavioural model provides the best insight into human behavioural styles that totally aligns to the DISC model, and also reflects the natural cycle of a business.

Accepting that a person can have two dominating traits, such as D and I, if we look for another perspective it becomes evident that there is a DI style. This means that breaking down the four-trait DISC model gives you an eight-trait model (D-DI-I-IS-S-SC-C-DC). When we applied the model to a business context during our research, we recognised that each style had a specific value which it brought to the business, as shown below:

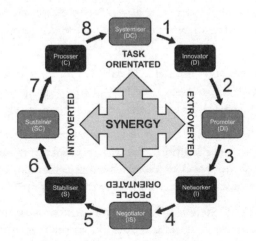

In analysing these eight profiles, it becomes clear how they complement one another, and where they most contribute value to the business and its evolutionary growth. The business cycle begins with innovation and creation. The eight profile types comprise:

- **Innovator** (DISC Style D) – this extrovert-oriented profile is an ambitious 'ideas' person who drives innovation. They think out of the box and can be dominating types by nature. They enjoy dynamic environments and welcome change. They like to start things, progress several activities at the same time and are very results-driven. They are naturally task-oriented people, and desire to lead and be in control.

- **Promoter** (DISC Style DI) – this extrovert-oriented profile positions themselves as a go-to person who ideally is an important person or has a key role to play. They are good at self-promotion and understand the power of branding. They need to be in a position where they can shine and be seen.

- **Networker** (DISC Style I) – this profile is the most extrovert-oriented style. They are friendly and like to engage with, and inspire others. They are good at connecting with others and are energised by people. They tend to have a wide circle of friends and are the most sociable of all the styles.

- **Negotiator** (DISC Style IS) – this profile is the most natural deal-maker, business developer, negotiator or seller of ideas who drives connections with others. It's a very people-oriented style that sits between introvert and extrovert, and they are easy people to deal with.

- **Stabiliser** (DISC Style S) – this introvert-oriented profile brings stability to the team. As a good listener and skilled at building relationships, they help solve team-related issues and become the glue to the team. Security is important to them, and trust in a relationship is critical for them.

- **Sustainer** (DISC Style SC) – this introvert-oriented profile looks towards sustainability both for the organisation and their own wealth. They are good at recognising the elements of long-term success, and picking assets that will grow over time.

- **Processor** (DISC Style C) – this profile is the most introvert-oriented style. They have high standards and like to make informed decisions.

They are 'details' people who strive to understand things at a deep level. Very capable of tackling tasks themselves, they prefer to work alone.

- **Systemiser** (DISC Style DC) – this profile is the ideal trouble-shooter, able to generate ideas and solve technical problems. They like to take a high-level view of an organisation and can recognise areas of improvement from a holistic systems perspective.

Operating in roles that fit each individual's personal profile is the ultimate career aim. It's where people can flow best and bring the most value to a business. Evidence that individuals are living in alignment within their flow includes being energised by what they do; using the least amount of energy to do their job; being passionate about their work; and having a sense of achievement and satisfaction about their output. It's about being truly happy with their role and feeling they are valued and are contributing.

The Extended DISC®[5] behavioural profiling tool is known to be the most accurate for identifying behavioural styles and potential flow states. It includes a graph which, by the lines that divide the quadrants and then further subdivides them, shows eight distinct styles. In fact, Extended DISC® recognises and reports on 40 different styles within each quadrant, with a total of 160 styles in all. This comprehensive analysis enables an in-depth distinction between individual traits.

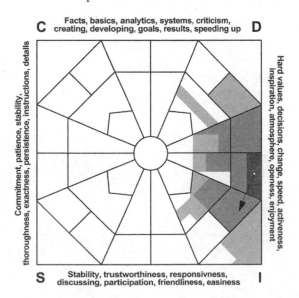

In the above example, the darkest shading shows that this person has an ID style, which we refer to as a promoter (Extended DISC® calls this an influencer). The shading also reveals what roles would benefit from being developed further, and also where investments in training would not be conducive to expanding on strengths. It's designed to identify areas that require more energy, which relate more to ebb (the white zones) for tasks that would likely better fit other individuals' styles in a team environment. Remember that in any role there will be tasks that utilise more energy, and others that use less, so it's not about avoiding the more strenuous tasks, but making sure that all tasks within the team are covered. Through this insight, leaders can ensure that they are not neglecting important areas such as planning, and it may also help them decide which tasks they can delegate.

Not only does its report format reveal an individual's core (natural) style, as shown in Profile II below, it also indicates the perceived need to adjust their style for the role and environment they are in (Profile I). The more the two graphs look the same, the more in flow they are. From the example below we can see that this person is living their style well, but as they are lower in Profile I than Profile II, they are not completely playing to their strengths (also shown by the arrow in the graph above). Based on the comparison between the two graphs below (natural v. perceived need to adjust), they are feeling the need to focus more on their I style and are suppressing their natural D style to cope with their present environment.

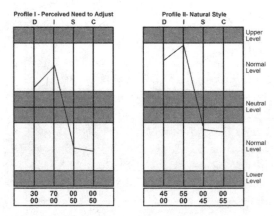

Completing this profile also shows where strengths need to be brought out in those who are lower in Profile I than Profile II, or reduced by those who are higher in Profile I than Profile II. It's the perfect coaching tool for getting into flow. In the example below, this person is not operating in flow, and the graph can be used to explain their current, adapted behavioural style in the workplace to guide changes that will better align with their natural strengths.

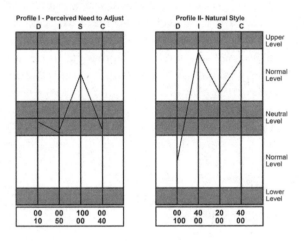

Some people may have never experienced operating in their natural strengths. They may have taken up career opportunities that were not strategically planned, but simply a consequence of the environment they were in or the people they associated with. Doing behavioural profiling early on, such as during your schooling years, will help a student discover their best educational and career paths.

Although developing natural strengths is critical to reaching the state of flow, sometimes weaknesses must be addressed too. Some of these are what we call supportive weaknesses that need to be developed to a lesser degree, to enable your strengths to flourish. For example, if a person is a business owner or operator, they'll require enough understanding of finance to be able to do their job properly. Financial details may not be in their flow, but are nonetheless important to support their role as leader.

Building on natural talents and understanding weaknesses gives greater awareness of oneself and others as we progress and as new team members are introduced.

Identifying the right person to join an existing team requires skill and knowledge to ensure the right fit, because the cost of hiring the wrong person has a dramatic effect on many areas of the organisation and impacts productivity, often in hidden and substantial ways.

Team profiling reveals how the group will work together as a team, as well as highlighting any pressures on the team that offer feedback on the prevailing culture. Take the example of the team below, where the dots show each individual's core style, and then on the graph on the right it plots the overall sum of the dominating traits into a single graph. In this particular example, the team is a sales department and you can see they have similar behavioural traits. More importantly, the grouping shows areas not covered by main strengths and, in this case, low in the 'C' technical traits. In fact the shaded graph shows low strengths in the improver, systemiser and innovator blends. The whitened areas suggest skills that demand more energy from the team members, and these are therefore often areas of low skill, or where tasks may be being avoided.

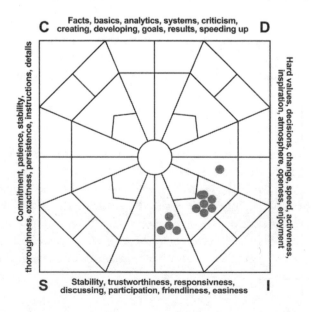

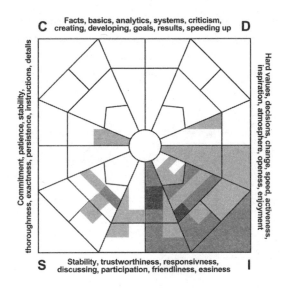

The influences on the individuals to adjust their behavioural style to cope with their new environment often indicates the cultural challenges by the length and direction of the arrows that appear when comparing their core styles to their adjusted styles. Based on the graph below, the individuals have adapted their core styles towards different areas from their core blends.

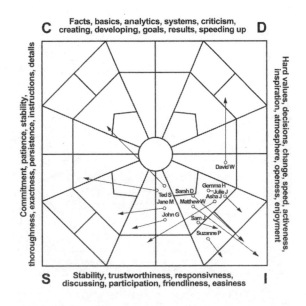

Where the team members are not occupying the same type of roles, the traits of the team will be more spread out as in the sample below but, again, this identifies areas that are not well covered. These often become focus skills for recruitment. The aim is to ideally select a team where all behavoural traits are covered.

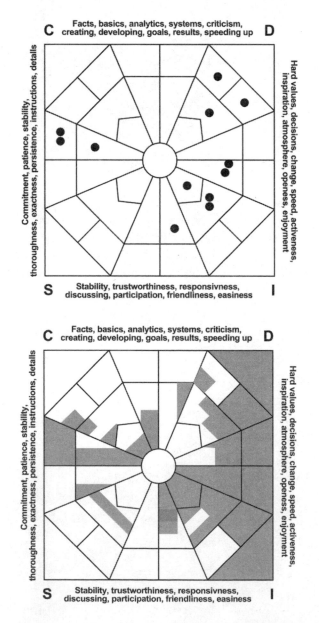

The diagram below provides an example of the obvious cultural influences on the team, because the arrows, which depict the individuals' perceived need to adjust, largely point towards the same areas. This example represents a sales team that was required to be more interfacing with people.

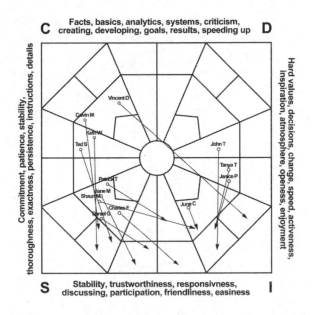

These types of tools are invaluable in providing in-depth insights into how a manager or leader can support team members to achieve their flow and how to recognise areas of improvement. It helps the individual team members understand their key strengths, and those of their teams, as well as the pressures on the individuals and the team to adjust.

Aim to support the team in their flow and avoid adjusting oneself or the team away from where the core natural talents lie. An evolving leader should surround themselves with people with different behavioural traits and be respectful of their talents. The objective is to get every team member recognising their talents and to contribute to the team in a harmonious way with the other behavioural blends of the group.

KEY LESSONS

1. Every person has a core behavioural style which represents their natural talents.
2. These natural gifts reveal the individual's potential for greatness.
3. The state of flow is not natural, and on average it takes some 10,000 hours of training, education and experience to reach a level of mastery or expertise, but this process is faster when you align your talents with your natural behavioural style.
4. When people are in their flow they produce more results and are happier in the workplace.
5. When people are in their ebb, tasks take more energy and become exhausting.
6. An organisation's greatest asset is the people so great care and education must be applied when selecting new members of a team to ensure they are a correct fit for the existing team culture.
7. One person can destroy a productive team culture if that person is the wrong fit for the existing team. The best hiring skills must be utilised to assure that existing relationships are preserved, productive and sustained.
8. Behavioural styles are a blend between people and task orientation, and between introvert and extrovert orientation.
9. There is no universal common sense – we interpret common sense as where we share similar behavioural traits with others.
10. Behavioural profiling is the fastest way to identify a flow state and to discover how you can excel and what areas you should focus on.
11. Team behavioural profiling can demonstrate cultural influences and how well the team members are adjusting their behaviour to blend well with the group.

1. Tuckman, B. (1965). "Developmental sequence in small groups." *Psychological Bulletin* 63 (6): 384–99. doi:10.1037/h0022100. PMID 14314073.

2. Gladwell, M. (2011). *Outliers: The Story of Success*, Back Bay Books.

3. Gordon Training International, "Learning a New Skill is Easier Said than Done." Gordon Training International http://www.gordontraining.com/free-workplace-articles/learning-a-new-skill-is-easier-said-than-done/, accessed 22 November 2013.

4. Extended DISC (2013). http://www.extendeddisc.com/

5. Ibid.

Chapter 4

Ensuring Corporate Happiness

OVERVIEW

- Identify the ultimate purpose for everyone – happiness.
- Build this understanding into the fabric of organisational culture.
- Recognise that 'purpose' is the factor that aligns everybody and should be explicitly declared.
- Purpose is the ultimate motivator – knowing who you are and what you stand for creates inspired action.
- Recognise that passion, purpose, immersion and reflection are core contributors to happiness.

When businessman John Spedan Lewis took full control of the family business on his father's death in 1928, he already had a clear vision of how things should be run.[1] By 1907, he had already been given a quarter share of the business and was well on his way to heading up a significant division of the operation. He was only 21 years old. During this period, he became aware that he, his brother and his father (John

Lewis) were between them earning as much as the entire workforce. The seeds of some radical ideas were forming, although he was not able to develop these ideas further until he had a serious fall from his horse and had to convalesce for some time.

The 'happiness' of his employees was right at the centre of his thinking. As soon as he returned to work he began to experiment with new systems of working. He shortened the working day, he set up staff committees and he provided a third week's paid holiday, which was an innovation in the retail sector at the time. His father disagreed with the young Spedan's radical ideas and the two fell out, leading to the father running one part of the business and the son the other.

The son's management style turned his side of the business from a £8,000 deficit into a £20,000 profit in a few short years. His ideas were working and showing great promise. By the time John Lewis senior died in 1928, the son's vision was clear. The following year he created the first Constitution for John Lewis Partnership Limited and signed the first Trust Settlement that effectively gave him practical control, but allowed profits to be distributed among the employees. Twenty-one years later, the second Trust Settlement was signed and the Partnership became the property of the people employed within it.

Establishing the value of 'happiness' at the core of an organisation's mission and purpose is one of the essential hall marks of a humanistic business. Today, the John Lewis Partnership still has the Constitution its founder created at the centre of its operation. 'The happiness of its members' is the Partnership's ultimate purpose and you can't help but feel the tangible effect of this aim wherever you come into contact with any one of their Partners. In 2013, the group's gross sales were in excess of £9.5 billion and the 84,700 partners each received a 17 per cent bonus on top of their salary. Not bad for a focus on happiness!

Examining areas such as wellbeing and happiness reveals interesting research done in this area. It includes objective as well as subjective areas of life experiences and there are some clear links between wellbeing, health and happiness that provide identifiable incentives for individuals and the organisations in which they work. Individuals demonstrating greater positivity and optimism have been shown to have better health, fewer serious illnesses and less time off work. A study by the University of Kentucky[2] showed a direct link between individuals' happiness and longevity, using 180 Catholic nuns who lived in a convent. Researchers chose nuns for the experiment because they lead very similar lifestyles, thus eliminating other potentially confusing variables found in the normal population. The study showed that the nuns who demonstrated happiness and positivity in their behaviour and language lived on average 10 years longer than those who were considered unhappy or negative. Now, that's got to be a worthwhile incentive!

Studies identify 'top-down' and 'bottom-up' theories of wellbeing. The top-down aspects tend to be those that relate to internal factors such as genetic predispositions and personality. The bottom-up aspects tend to relate more to external factors, such as experiences and environmental influences. There is some evidence that the former – the internal set-points – have a greater effect on how individuals assess health, happiness and performance than the external factors, but both need managing if personal potential is to be reached. It's interesting that much of the research about human behaviour and thinking started by exploring individuals with mental illness, weakness and damage, later focusing on the strategies which helped those individuals to reintegrate and become 'normally' functioning members of society. In his book, *Authentic Happiness*,[3] the psychologist and former president of the American Psychological Association, Martin Seligman, claimed: 'For the last half century psychology has been consumed with a single topic only – mental illness.' Perhaps it is not too difficult to see how this process of taking performance from 'below the line' and aiming for 'normal' can influence other aspects of people's thinking and behaviour. If this is the reference framework for how standards are set, then the best that can be achieved is zero! In fact, industry benchmarks are effectively based on the average and not the excellent. In terms of the standards for humanistic businesses that we are proposing, setting the bar much higher is about focusing on excellence not mediocrity.

This process relates to those areas of personal performance and experience that represent peak states of human endeavour, such as ecstasy, optimal performance, great inner clarity and flow. It's worth recognising that different skills are required to manage performance above the line, compared to those that start below the line and aim towards the norm. This is the difference between therapy and coaching, as each has a completely different intent and aim. Where the measure of success is set will drive different behaviours in order to achieve that end. John Spedan Lewis was enlightened enough over a century ago to realise that aiming at 'the happiness of its members' would drive the structure and culture of the whole organisation to align behind this aim.

> *'I've always wanted to be successful. My definition of being successful is contributing something to the world . . . and being happy while doing it . . . You have to enjoy what you are doing. You won't be very good if you don't. And secondly, you have to feel that you are contributing something worthwhile . . . if either of these ingredients are absent, there's probably some lack of meaning in your work.'*
>
> Norman Augustine, former CEO of Lockheed Martin[4]

How the measure of success is determined is an important part of the discussion about happiness and whether that reference point is inside or outside of the individual. Athletes aim to be better than their competitors, but really the aim is to be better individually and exceed beyond that individual's personal best. It is different ways of looking at it, with the same ultimate goal to win. The calibration of personal optimum performance must be based upon an internal reference point, one that is related to personal values as well as natural potential. Happiness is related to the satisfaction of those fundamental values. In fact, happiness is an outcome of a journey. It is a sense of being, a state of recognition. Reaching the peak of a mountain is in recognising the difficulty of the climb: the exhilaration of the achievement, the sense of progress and the realisation of the progress.

When an organisation invests in its human equity a fundamental human need is being addressed that moves us and motivates us to excel beyond mediocrity into excellence. The investment in the happiness of stakeholders results in higher performance, greater productivity, improved culture and increasing profits.

One of the great thinkers in the field of human behaviour, the late Abraham Maslow, identified the evolutionary stages that human beings undergo as they mature and move towards self-actualisation. If this journey is to be undertaken, then we need to move beyond the drive towards security alone. We must swallow the beast of insecurity if you will, ensuring that it is digested, and in doing so we absorb its power. So much of the definition of security in life is entwined with money. There has been much research on this subject – in fact there is a whole field of study entitled: happiness economics. Despite our commonly held beliefs about wealth being able to bring us happiness, it seems that most studies refute this idea of money being a motivator for our experience of joy and fulfilment. Money certainly enables the ability to choose what is done with our time and wealth. A greed-based focus or love of money may bring down individuals, but a respect for it as a tool for good seems to be a critical aspect of those who are sustainably wealthy.

In polls taken by the National Opinion Research Centre at the University of Chicago, about a third of Americans said they were really happy back in 1950. Since then, the polls have been taken periodically, and the results have stayed about the same, despite individual wealth increasing by roughly a factor of three over the same period. In their article entitled 'From wealth to wellbeing? Money matters, but less than people think', the authors found that once basic needs are met (after earning over US$75,000 in the study conducted in the US), then it ceased to contribute to happiness.[5]

The study also found that people tend to overestimate the influence of wealth on happiness by 100 per cent. There is this relationship of diminishing returns whereby once our personal wealth passes a threshold and our inherent needs are satisfied, it seems it doesn't increase happiness. In fact, Richard Easterlin, Professor of Economics at the University of Southern California, stated that job satisfaction does not depend upon salary and that having extra money did not contribute towards happiness as much as enjoying one's job or one's social network.[6] There are also some studies on lottery winners that find happiness levels increase after the event, but return to 'base-line' levels within a period of about three months to a year. Knowing what doesn't create happiness in our work environment is of course only part of the story. If an organisation's interests are about driving extraordinary performance, it is important to identify the positive contributors.

The area of positive psychology is a relatively recent field and was developed by Martin Seligman and Mihaly Csikszentmihályi around 1998[7] with the aim 'to find and nurture genius and talent' and 'to make normal life more fulfilling'. Its research, rather than focusing on pathology, looks at strength, virtue, success and happiness. It is an area that is very much interested in happiness and personal peak performance and includes an examination of positive emotions, individual traits and institutions.

Csíkszentmihályi summarises positive psychology's[8] findings by describing three platforms that must be present for happiness to occur: Pleasure, Meaning and Engagement. In context, they are very similar to the three motivating factors that author Daniel Pink describes as being Autonomy, Purpose and Mastery.[9] Based on Csikszentmihalyi's model, we found that these were similarly Passion, Purpose, Immersion and Reflection.

Passion

When a person is in their flow they are in a state of passion. When in flow an individual can complete tasks seemingly effortlessly compared to others, because their starting point is based on passion. Passion is easier to recognise at the end of the spectrum when an individual expresses excitement, drive and aliveness.

Passion therefore ranges from that short-term, perhaps somewhat superficial satisfaction, to the state of enjoyment which implies a deeper connection with those things that speak to inner needs, interests and desires. It is to do with those things with which people are programmed to satisfy themselves, including food, security and health. These include those physiological and safety needs, described earlier by Maslow, that are not huge motivators beyond the point of satisfaction. Csikszentmihályi seems to verify this when he states that this area is the lowest indicator of individual happiness.

Despite this, passion is an area to which some organisations pay great attention and, rightly, one that should be well managed. The John Lewis Partnership is a good example of structuring remuneration appropriately so that effort and reward are directly linked. Despite the motivational limitations of money as described above, if there is no correlation between effort and reward, or the level of remuneration does not satisfy personal needs, then it becomes a source of total demotivation.

In his book, *Stumbling on Happiness*,[10] psychologist Daniel Gilbert describes research which suggests that money makes a significant difference to the poor, but has a greatly diminished effect once one reaches middle class. Gilbert is therefore adamant that people should figure out what jobs they really enjoy and then find ways of doing those jobs for a living.

This is consistent with our research that when natural talents are aligned with passion that leads to a state of flow where performance improves and efficiency increases. Malcolm Gladwell's 10,000-hour rule, described earlier, suggests that a person needs around 10,000 hours of education, development and practice to reach the state of a master or expert. We agree, as evidence is showing that a person's natural behavioural-based growth potential has to be nurtured and developed before it is in a state of flow. Therefore, flow is not a natural state but rather a developed capability of high competency in an area of passion.

Some organisations go to great lengths to creatively satisfy some of our needs at this level, and the best organisations are good at blending play with work. The culture in Google, for example, is well known, and their list of employee perks include gyms and swimming pools, on-site gourmet chefs, physicians, hair stylists and dental services, video games, football and ping-pong as well as 'nap pods' for rest and rejuvenation. This links back to that sense of being important and nurtured, where the employee feels valued, and reciprocates with loyalty and a commitment to work.

Purpose

Csíkszentmihályi describes 'meaning' as a connection with those things that are greater than ourselves, including the experiencing of beauty, being absorbed in the abstract, or feeling part of a wider group, purpose or mission. There's some evidence that ministers of religion tend to be happier than the average person. This is not necessarily due to their belief in a greater power, but rather the sense of meaning and life purpose that their belief gives them. The connection with something that is bigger than them, which has some higher purpose and therefore relevant meaning, is what creates this state. This can be replicated in many professions.

When an organisation establishes a deeper purpose and becomes values driven the fundamental philosophy of positive engagement increases from all stakeholders.

Martin Seligman observes that there are two kinds of hospital orderly.[11] Their job, which includes cleaning out patients' bedpans, has a high degree of repetition, as well as a low social status. One type of orderly sees the job as a means of paying the bills and can't wait to finish work and retire. The other is somebody who sees themselves as part of a wider organisation which cares for patients. The shift of their focus is key. It comes from noticing that some people focus on the actual task, some on the short-term wins and others on the ultimate outcome.

The orderlies in the latter group see part of their job as contributing to make things easier for the doctors and nurses and improving the patients' experience. They are the kind of people who will bring in flowers for patients or put up pictures on the walls so that the first thing a recovering patient will see is a pleasant scene in front of them. This sense of connection does not have to be attributed to some supernatural power; rather it represents something that gives their daily activity meaning and purpose.

Consistent with our observation of the new era of business, a humanistic business must look beyond the confines of its own operation and see itself as part of a greater, wider organism. This sense of belonging speaks to all of us and must be replicated in our business community. The culture and leadership in any organisation must have the awareness and the courage to look beyond mere survival and towards the satisfaction of the wider interests of the organisation. It must deliberately develop those deeper processes that nurture optimal performance, self-actualisation and service. This sets the bar high, but the rewards are worth the investment. The optimum position is to have people connected with a movement rather than a task. They become part of the whole, having a sense of connection, and contributing to the ultimate effect of being a contributor to a community, where their inclusion has a deeper reason linked to greater good.

Immersion

According to Csikszentmihályi's research, engagement is the platform most predictive of happiness and performance. He and his colleagues conducted in excess of 8,000 interviews of people in many professions and cultures and with varying levels of education, but who all experienced a particular state that was characterised by total engagement in a task, as well as feelings of ecstasy and timelessness. Many of the people interviewed were in creative professions, such as artists and scientists, doing jobs which did not necessarily provide great financial reward, while others were business leaders. However, this state of absorbed engagement was common to all. Many of the interviewees used an analogy of the flow of water to describe the state of creative impulse they were experiencing and it's this description that he used to name this state of flow. Csikszentmihályi lists the following attributes as descriptors of the state of flow:[12]

1. Completely involved in what we are doing – totally focused and absolute concentration.

2. A sense of ecstasy – of being outside everyday reality.

3. Great inner clarity – knowing what needs to be done, and how well we are doing it.

4. Knowing that the activity is doable – that our skills are adequate to the task.

5. A sense of serenity – no worries about oneself, and a feeling of growing beyond the boundaries of the ego.

6. Timelessness – thoroughly focused on the present, hours seem to pass by in minutes.

7. Intrinsic motivation – whatever produces flow becomes its own reward.

Ecstasy may seem like an unusual word, but Csikszentmihályi notes that the word comes from the Greek root meaning 'to step aside'. In other words, it is an altered state of consciousness whereby one's own existence is temporarily suspended where there is a sense of observer in the activity and not the participant.

Neuroscience says human beings process approximately 134 bits of information per second, and that listening to one person speak takes up around 60 bits of information per second. If there is full absorption in a task, then there is no spare capacity available for individuals to process anything else, and this state of suspended awareness occurs. Musicians describe 'watching their hands', almost as an out of body experience and in a state of wonder. Writers talk about ideas coming spontaneously to them and being an observer as the words form on the page. Many individuals could sit and look at their hands and perhaps the blank screen in front of them for hours, perhaps days, and not experience that state of ecstasy, wonder and spontaneous creativity that is being in flow. It seems that coupled with mental and environmental conditions, people need another ingredient that is known as skill.

According to Csikszentmihályi, it takes 10 years[13] or more to achieve this, while Malcolm Gladwell talks about the 10,000 hours it takes for this level of mastery to occur and thereby create something that has not been created before. So, what has this to do with happiness? Our interest here is in creating the conditions for anyone to perform at their optimum while being in a state of joy. Although some of the research focused on extraordinary performers, it also looked at others who achieved exactly the same state of consciousness, but were undertaking less grand tasks.

The research concluded that this state of flow was available to everyone given the right conditions, but once this state of engagement is experienced, extraordinary performance can occur. The same state is described in different ways depending on the occupation. Software developers talk about getting into 'the zone' or 'hack mode', when creativity reaches an undistracted state. Stock market traders talk about being 'in the pipe' to describe this psychological state of flow when trading during high-volume days and market corrections. Professional poker players use the term 'playing the A-game', while pool players often refer to it as being in 'dead stroke'.

Although a flow state can be entered while performing any activity, it's most likely to occur when the individual is totally engaged in a task or activity for intrinsic purposes. Passive activities don't usually create flow experiences as the individual has to be 'active' to enter the state. There are three conditions that have to be met to achieve a flow state: clarity of goals; specific and instant feedback; and match challenge and capacity, as detailed below.

Goals	• Have clarity in your goals
Feedback	• Get specific and instant feedback
Emotional State	• Match the challenge and capacity
STATE OF FLOW	

1. Goals – Have clarity in your goals

This refers to identifying the immediate next step rather than the totality of the overall objective. If an individual is a musician, it's not about completing the piece, but playing the next note. If a climber, it's not about reaching the top, but where to find the next hold for the hand or foot. The pathway needs to be crystal clear for the pathway to be induced. It is anchored in the moment which gives momentum and direction to the future.

Senior levels of management are often clear about objectives and purpose, but often this clarity does not filter down to those in the field, so this clarity and focus needs to be extended through all levels. To create motivation and positive engagement individuals must be aligned to the vision and understand how their role directly contributes to its fulfilment.

2. Feedback – Get specific and instant feedback

There are many areas of life when learning happens organically and naturally, receiving specific, often instant feedback that makes the experience effective and often joyful. For example, when children learn to walk they have a real sense of mission for the task. Their specific, instant feedback is in the act of falling over. They know exactly where they are in relation to their goals and they have a very clear idea of what to do next.

Equally, with certain competitive sporting activities, athletes are entirely engaged in feeling the strain of their own resources being tested, feeling their limits and experiencing the response from opponents. These endeavours often link to instant, unmistakable feedback from others in the field of play. If an athlete is not fast enough, they get caught, and if the opponent is faster, he or she gets to score. There is immediate feedback on what works and what doesn't. The responses are managed by experience, not some idealised view from the sidelines. An athlete develops their performance through direct feedback and adapting to that feedback to improve performance. A Humanistic organisation that is serious about performance, reads the feedback from internal and external stakeholders alike, then develops a strategy that will produce results through focusing upon meeting the foundational needs of its key players, being value and purpose driven and operating from a strategic plan.

3. Emotional State – Match the challenge and capacity

The research on flow theory makes a direct correlation between feelings and challenge. It states that there is an optimum relationship between how challenging a particular task is and how skilled individuals are at managing it. The state of flow is between having a sense of control and the feeling of arousal. Not too dissimilar is the knowledge that people need a level of stress to get into action, yet too much stress leads to deterioration of individual wellbeing.

Based on flow theory, human beings gain the most enjoyment from circumstances under which they are stretched and challenged just beyond their current level of capacity compared to the challenge. There is much evidence in life that suggests people get better and better at being better through stretching just beyond their level of comfort and skill. Twenty years ago if a car managed to last for 50,000 miles people were delighted. Today, it's common for cars to last for over 200,000 miles. Domestic appliances are more energy-efficient than they were only a few years ago. Sports performance targets are increasing with new records being set each year.

Csikszentmihályi suggests that this intrinsic link between what we find most enjoyable and challenging is what differentiates us from other species and is one of the key factors why we have evolved so dramatically. It is perhaps important to state that this improvement in performance is also to do with the fact that modern performers, whether in sports, science or design, train themselves more effectively. In his book *Talent is Overrated: what really separates world-class performers from everybody else,*[14] Geoff Colvin describes the process of exceptional performance as being less to do with innate talent and more to do with what he calls 'deliberate practice'. This is a highly targeted form of training which directly and indirectly enhances performance in a particular field. We are changing the way we measure and create high-performing individuals.

Taking all this information together, the implications for high-performing organisations start to become clearer. It's the job of the individuals within the organisation to identify and apply their natural gifts and it's the job of the environment and culture to not only help this process of identification, but also to nurture, develop and enhance its application. Martin Seligman says it's about '. . . using your signature strengths every day to produce authentic happiness and abundant gratification'.[15]

Despite understanding the science behind enhanced performance, it seems that many organisations are structured to resist its application. For example, if individuals need to be operating in the range where they are challenged at just the right level for growth and optimum perform-ance to occur, they need a role that is just beyond their current ability. Due to the pressure and constraints placed upon them, most compa-nies are more likely to put people in positions where they are experienced and have a proven track record. They will place them according to what they are good at, not necessarily what they need to work on. The best organisations will recognise this need and seek creative means to apply these challenges.

In summary, immersion in the context of happiness and at its highest point is the state of total absorption, of intense focus where the brain is totally present and there is a sense of participation where the task is the focal point of the whole being. It evokes our senses to be on high arousal and alert, like the race-car driver feeling the pedals, the steering wheel, the gears and with an intense concentration on the track. It is where all parts are working as one, in sync, and for a single purpose.

Reflection

Any continuous improvement process needs review and feedback. Reflection has two parts: firstly to measure progress to enable necessary changes to the path of success and, secondly, the need to celebrate wins and recognise the journey, its stages and its end.

The first part is about being persistent, to overcome the challenges found when embarking on any new path, to recognise that all paths have highs and lows and to enable a checking process that ensures quality control is in place. This reflection mechanism is about review-ing progress to recognise the current position and make any necessary adjustments. It also includes questioning if the end result is still rele-vant and the best option. There is always the challenge of climbing the ladder of success only to find out it is leaning on the wrong building.

Leaders need to listen to others, and sometimes that means changing a decision for the betterment of the organisation. This may bruise the ego in the short term, but shows true leadership in recognising that change may be inevitable in order to gain the best possible results. At the beginning of the journey there are many unknowns. The path that is chosen is based on the information available at the time, and the resources that are accessible. As the target nears, uncertainty decreases and the risks become apparent. This recognises that additional information, new learning and insights may require an adjustment to established plans. In project management terminology this is called change or variation management. True leaders recognise the need to make timely decisions, but those decisions may have to be revisited and adjusted, based on the feedback and other inputs they receive.

The second part is recognising the journey itself. All paths have obstacles, disruptions and challenges to overcome, and happiness seems to be more apparent to those who take the time to reflect and recognise the path already travelled. This means that all project completions should be celebrated, even if it's just a drink, a cake or a social get-together. Projects that involve more risk to life, isolation or unpleasant duties (like cleaning up after a disaster involving loss of human life) may require some form of counselling or additional support at their conclusion. Recognising and honouring the end sometimes brings better closure to the team, and therefore better wellbeing. The most dramatic of projects will be those linked to high risk or loss of human life, which reaffirms the importance of the humanistic side of our interactions.

Many people go from one project to another, one accomplishment to another, one qualification to another without stopping and reflecting, often chasing success without any breath. Not appreciating the wins along the way often creates stress and a sense of never getting there. Such people miss living in the moment, and they may be missing a lot more by not connecting more deeply with others and sharing that moment of necessary reflection, looking back with amazement, and a sense of adventure and accomplishment.

Reflection, whether it be in the form of a quality check, a review, feedback, a celebration or just a ponderous thought, is an important aspect of personal and team growth. Don't discount its importance, noting that some behavioural styles need it more than others. Learn to stop, breathe, smell the roses, but most importantly reflect on the steps that have been taken to obtain the results that are apparent today.

The Currency of Happiness

It is believed that passion, purpose, immersion and reflection can all exist separately. The magic is when all four are consciously integrated and practised, and that is where the alchemy occurs. Some practical ideas for integrating happiness and creating that alchemy include the following.

Provide clarity

Be clear about personal purpose, personal values and personal goals, both for the individual and the organisation. Only by making the purpose visionary is it possible to create something new. John Spedan Lewis's purpose of the 'happiness of its members' is still visionary today and must have been utterly unique over 100 years ago. At a recent talk,[16] Jimmy Wales, founder of Wikipedia, stated that a business must start with a moral purpose and stick to that throughout. This clarity and consistency are the building blocks for authenticity and integrity.

Match personal and organisational values

The greater the alignment between personal values and that of the organisation, the better the personal fit. Organisations tend to hire on talents and fire on misaligned values. The key is to be driven by passion and purpose. Even if the right fit occurs, the role should be challenging in the most positive way possible. People need to be in a lifelong learning environment where they are consciously alert and in a state of arousal.

At a recent talk, the Olympic hurdler Colin Jackson advised his audience to pick something they love to do when choosing a profession. If the individual aim is to be the best that is possible, it will involve a lot of hard work. If there is no passion or love for what a person does they will never stick to the course of success.

The late businesswoman and founder of The Body Shop, Anita Roddick,[17] once said:

> *'I want to work for a company that contributes to and is part of the community. I want something not just to invest in. I want something to believe in.'*

Give people detailed, specific and regular feedback

People need to know how they contribute to the bigger picture, but specifically how they do that and how well they are doing in working towards meeting that end. This does not translate into greater supervision. Often in humanistic businesses, greater clarity of purpose and values means less structure and more personal responsibility and empowerment. Complexity is not always the answer to difficult problems. Having the courage to impose less structure creates greater autonomy and people will often rise to the challenge by raising their personal awareness and responsibility. Management and leadership styles may have to be adjusted and traditional hierarchies and job titles reviewed. Empowerment does require boundaries to be set by the leaders, but it enables creativity and a sense of personal power within those constraints, which are established to keep all energy equity aligned with the organisation's needs and away from personal agendas.

Link effort to reward

People need to know they make a difference and that they can influence their own future through their own endeavours. So make remuneration systems transparent, fair and related to performance. Although this can extend to bonus payments, pensions and other benefits, this doesn't have to be limited to money. Be creative about how reward is defined. If flow theory is right, then human beings are an inherently growth-orientated species. By including extracurricular experiences and training any improvement will eventually translate into performance.

People will gravitate towards rewards that are perceived as greater value, rather than money. Take the example of the single parent who might prefer to have the time to drop their child off and pick them up from school over extra pay in their pocket. Value is perceived differently for everyone, and there is no single reward that suits all. It's about knowing the individual, their needs and desires and how best to attract and support them.

Match challenge and skills

Help to expand people's skills and capabilities. Stretch them for their own growth. Support this growth in the workplace by understanding your people well enough to create the right circumstances for flow to occur. This is often achieved through behavioural profiling where you come to know where their natural talents lie and how they can be developed. Have a structure that is flexible enough to accommodate variety and encourage growth opportunities. Make sure it's transparent enough so that individuals know where they are in terms of their own skills and performance. This kind of culture engenders trust and respect that are the cornerstones of optimum happiness and performance.

Manage the environment

Recognise the need for pleasure and stress relief. Blend work and play effectively and create an environment that supports creativity, innovation and happiness. Consider creative spatial arrangements in the workplace that are open and flexible, noting that behavioural styles will influence the individual's desire for more quiet or noisy environments. Provide practical experiences such as meditation, visualisation and exercise. Make sure team members are given the correct resources, guidance and mentorship.

Become a business and a person who is easy to deal with. Learn about business systems and processes and how they support the business, remembering that process guides behaviour.

All these factors help create a positive, supportive and growth potential environment. In his book *Good Business: Leadership, Flow and the Making of Meaning*, Mihaly Csíkszentmihályi says:

> '. . . getting employees to give their best does not mean exploiting their talents as a means of generating higher profits. It is first and foremost a way to make it possible for them to grow as individuals, thus contributing to the true bottom line, which is to enhance happiness.'

Happy people attract and influence happy customers. Become the person you would want serving you.

Key Lessons

1. The heart of corporate happiness can be divided into four simple ingredients: Passion, Purpose, Immersion and Reflection.
2. Individual happiness is created when people are utilising their natural talents and acting within their natural flow.
3. The three conditions that must be present to achieve the state of flow are: clarity of goals, specific instant feedback and matching challenge and capacity.
4. A sense of meaning and connection is fundamental to corporate happiness. Daily activities need to be defined with clarity about how these daily tasks intersect in the overall systems that support the vibrancy of the organisation.
5. Human beings gain the most enjoyment from their roles when they are being stretched and challenged just beyond their current level.
6. Senior management are often clear about the objectives and purpose, but this clarity rarely filters down the levels of the rank and files to the rest of the organisation.
7. Money is rarely the motivator that drives the quest for happiness.

1. http://www.johnlewispartnership.co.uk/about/our-founder.html

2. Diener, E. (2008). *Happiness: unlocking the mysteries of psychological wealth*. Malden, MA: Blackwell Pub.

3. Seligman, Martin *Authentic Happiness: Using the New Positive Psychology to Realize Your Potential for Lasting Fulfillment*. New York: Free Press. ISBN 0-7432-2297-0. (Paperback edition, Free Press, 2004, ISBN 0-7432-2298-9)

4. Quoted by Mihaly Csiksentmihaly during a lecture on Flow: the secret to happiness in 2004. http://www.youtube.com/watch?v=fXIeFJCqsPs

5. Holmes, B. (7 September 2010) "Money can buy you happiness – up to a point." *New Scientist*.

6. Easterlin, R. (2008). "Income and happiness: towards a unified theory." *The Economic Journal*, 11(473), 465–484.

7. Seligman, Martin E.P.; Csikszentmihalyi, Mihaly (2000). "Positive Psychology: An Introduction." *American Psychologist* 55 (1): 5–14.

8. Ibid.

9. Pink, Daniel H. (2010). *Drive – The Surprising Truth about what motivates us*. 2815 of 3967: Canongate Books. ISBN 978-1-84767-888-1.

10. Gilbert, Daniel (2006). *Stumbling on Happiness*, Knopf, ISBN 1-4000-4266-6

11. Allan Gregg in conversation, with Martin Seligman, talking about 'Authentic Happiness,' http://www.youtube.com/watch?v=6QxZvBcz2BY

12. Csikszentmihalyi, M. (1990). *Flow: The Psychology of Optimal Experience*. New York: Harper and Row.

13. M. Csikszentmihaly, *Flow, the secret to happiness* TED talk, http://www.youtube.com/watch?v=fXIeFJCqsPs

14. Colvin, G. (2010) *Talent is Overrated: what really separates world-class performers from everybody else*, Portfolio Press.

15. Seligman, M.E.P. (2002). Authentic Happiness. New York: Free Press.

16. Community Dinner, Church of the Annunciation, Marble Arch, London, 2013.

17. http://www.brainyquote.com/quotes/authors/a/anita_roddick.html

Chapter 5

Driving Innovation

OVERVIEW
- Vision enables forward thinking that sees new ways of doing business, opportunities in creating and leveraging markets, innovation in products and improvements in business processes.
- Businesses follow natural cycles for growth.
- These business cycles align with personal behavioural strengths that enable individuals to contribute directly to growing the business.
- There are a number of innovation and thinking strategies which enable a business to create new products and services and reinvent themselves.

Although humanistic businesses tend to be flexible in their organisational structures, their team members have a great sense of clarity about their roles and responsibilities. This flexible structure, which combines fluidity and clarity, tends to inspire a mind-set of accountability and a desire for problem-solving and innovation. When the organisational structure allows for greater responsibility, the team members seem to step up to the role. The less hierarchy, the more personal responsibility for outcomes, and this seems to drive an internal entrepreneurial spirit that may be referred to as intrepreneurship. This kind of innovation supports the creation of new ideas, products and services.

All businesses begin by acting on an idea or original concept that triggers the business growth cycle described below. This whole cycle starts with innovation, and although every person can contribute to innovative thinking, some behavioural styles are more natural innovators. They think 'right out of the box' and can sometimes conceive quite unrealistic ideas that then rely on others to turn their ideas into doable solutions. These are the people who asked why their desktop computer couldn't be taken home, leading to the innovation of the laptop, or why they couldn't hold a computer in their hands, leading to the personal handheld digital assistant technology. They may not have the technical skill to make it happen, but they certainly have the ability to stretch team thinking and engage those who can.

Even though the Innovator has natural creativity, all styles contribute to innovation in their own ways. Negotiators innovate in their negotiations, and Processors innovate through process improvement. It's about knowing what value each individual can contribute. For each behavioural style there is a corresponding business growth cycle phase where their particular skills are most needed. The natural cycle of a business begins with the Innovation stage. During this phase, the Innovator behavioural profile comes in most handy, and their flow is critical to the business's success. While this doesn't mean you need an Innovator on the team, you will generally need one as a board director, mentor, coach, advisor or consultant if you want to fast-track your business's success.

There are eight business growth cycles which highlight the need to emphasise a particular strength where a specific behavioural style adds most value and has an important part to play. Each function of the organisation should be operating at the same time, so it's not about the business simply going from one growth stage to the next, but the focus of the leadership in allocating its time and business resources while the organisation is running its normal business. The business still needs to market itself, it still needs to sell and it still needs to deliver and improve. By identifying what key phase the business is in, one can utilise key people's strengths strategically in pre-empting the needs of the organisation. But when an organisation is in a particular stage, they must make sure they have the right balance of skills in the team to do it properly.

The eight-phase business growth cycle is shown below:

Organisations operate within these business growth cycles naturally, and they can evolve with each iteration across the full eight-stage cycle. When analysing any business, it becomes clear at what stage of their evolution they are, and therefore one can predict and prepare them for the coming phase. This enables a strategic and focused management control of the intensity and duration of each stage. For example, the cost of refinement in the Improving phase can lead to cash-flow issues if this phase is prolonged and, at worst case, the cost of improving it in preparation for the market can lead to bankruptcy. This reinforces the importance of progressing this natural cycle so that one can gain the advantage of improvement without overdoing it. Perfecting a product keeps it in research and development, but it's vital to know when enough is enough to get the product released and sales coming in the door.

The Innovating stage of the cycle is where the business idea results in a business start-up or a new product being developed. The business then needs to build up its Branding and profile to gain market awareness and presence of a trade name. This may include the branding of a new product coming online.

The Networking stage is where the brand name spreads to the right people who create the distribution channels or market interest in preparation for the selling phase. The target market is identified or a new one created.

All businesses survive on revenue, and with its now trusted brand and targeted market awareness, it moves into the Selling phase where prospects are converted to clients. The aim is not to just have clients, but to retain them, as one of the traits of a humanistic business is that it excels in repeat business and referrals. After the sales phase, the focus is on delivery and supply. This is where the business enters the Stabilising phase, which aims to ensure it can consistently and in a timely manner meet the demand created and deliver on customers' expectations. Predictability in the brand is created, which reaffirms the trust in the business from the client's perspective.

To ensure the business continues year after year, sustainability is required. The Sustaining phase looks at the investments of the business – how profits are often retained and invested into assets and wealth is grown. Sometimes this links to growing the business into a franchise model or into a global business of related companies. Sustainability requires both consistency of cash flow and the inclusion of passive revenue generation through franchising, reselling, licensing or investments that provide dividends.

Next comes process improvement, which helps reduce the risk of relying on key people by making sure the right systems and processes are in place and start to run the business and guide behaviour. In this way we get refinement and the business has intellectual property over the dependence on its critical people. This is an important phase for creating a franchise business system, as well as for improving products and maximising efficiencies in systems, processes and practices.

Systemising takes a more helicopter-level view in seeing the gaps between the people, systems and processes and their interrelationships and integration needs. It goes beyond process to looking at a holistic relationship between all the business forces. It aims at fixing the whole business by addressing the areas that have been causing the key challenges in order to make it work like a highly tuned machine. All aspects of the business are considered and the key hurts remedied once and for all. This is the completion stage and the end of the cycle.

Once this phase is completed and each of the elements working, it generates a new beginning and a new iteration of the cycle. The first cycle establishes the business, and repeating the cycle is about producing new products or services, or reinventing the business. A business that has survived many years, must reinvent itself, otherwise it will age and die, just like the human body must generate new cells to survive. This is why innovation is required. New products and services refresh the market's interest, which triggers a new era of sales. You either change and adapt to the moving market or you get left behind and lose your market position.

Once you understand the business growth cycle model, it becomes evident how and when the specialist skills of the individual behavioural styles come in most handy. Each behavioural profile aligns with one particular business cycle better than any other, which maintains the on-going and needed perspective in the business. This alignment is shown below, so that you can assess the key people you need in the business as each cycle approaches. Such people may include team members, external advisors, board directors, mentors, coaches or contractors.

Individual Profile	DISC Equivalent	Organisational Business Cycle
Innovator	D	Innovating – starting the business or driving new creative developments.
Promoter	DI	Branding – building a market profile and promoting the brand.
Networker	I	Networking – building brand awareness to a wider audience and market.
Negotiator	IS	Selling / Negotiating – Selling ideas or product, closing business and generating revenue.
Stabiliser	S	Stabilising – managing acquisitions and stabilising the team.
Sustainer	SC	Sustaining – bringing long-term sustainability and managing investments.
Processor	C	Processing – creating and improving processes and reducing the risk of the business relying on critical people to management through a process others can use.
Systemiser	DC	Systemising – taking a helicopter view of the business to look at improving the systems, including trouble-shooting key challenges.

At the beginning of the cycle, innovation brings together creativity, practicality and appropriateness into the business and is effectively the foundation for everything else. It drives the product design and service delivery ideas, as well as involving problem-solving. There are many tools that enable teams to shift their thinking paradigm and become more creative, which leads to the business as a whole positioning itself with a unique value proposition that differentiates itself from its competitors.

Given that competitors will later mimic and replicate what works well, it becomes apparent why the business growth cycle is needed. A business must keep innovating and reinventing to stay a leader in the marketplace. This often results in a business transforming into new areas, or new technologies.

Challenges to Innovative Thinking

Innovation is not only the start of the business growth cycle, it is the lifeline of a business. In understanding how to innovate and reinvent is to find the magic in the evolution of growth. There are three key challenges with how the brain works that naturally inhibit innovative thinking.

The first one relates to how the brain naturally prefers to use existing and frequently used neural-network paths. These pathways are created with new thoughts, and reaffirmed with repeat thoughts that keep re-firing and strengthening those same paths. It explains why repeated actions results in the creation of habits that represent the dominating pathways which force thinking a certain way, and why people tend to take the same route from home to work each day. People are creatures of habit, and therefore they can get caught in the same thinking patterns day after day due to these overpowering and dominating neural pathways that they have created and reinforced.

The second challenge relates to how sensory information is deleted, distorted and generalised before it goes into the human neurology. Earlier we mentioned the research of Mihaly Csikszentmihályi who suggests that our five senses (vision, hearing, touch, smell and taste) are being bombarded by approximately two million bits of information per second, and your nervous system's filters decrease this to a manageable size of about 134 bits per second to process the information. The actual amount of information you process is therefore approximately

0.000067 per cent of what you first received through your senses. This means that of the small percentage of the information individuals pick up through the sensors, over 99 per cent of that was lost in the brain's filtering system, noting that the sensors picked up only a small segment of the actual information available.

The information the brain finally let through was also modified according to the established values, beliefs and past experiences. The brain filters information based upon interest and focus. This means that a person's profession and personal interests will also sway their focus in any situation. Lawyers will tend to be focused on the commercial elements, and accountants on the financials. This explains why two business people in the same situation see different opportunities and take different messages away from the same exposure. Experiences are therefore subjective to one's own thoughts.

The third challenge also relates to the neurological filtering system, in that it favours known reference data that is already held in the memory. After a person has learnt what distinguishes the coloured, it is near impossible to be convinced it could be any other colour. Similarly people make associations to names of things that are undisputed truths in their own mind. The mind tends to use what it knows as the benchmark or reference point to work from. This can somewhat limit the 'out of box' thinking as the mind starts with what it knows to be true. Looking at that colour we call red, we already know that someone at some time came up with the concept that particular hue was to be called red, and we accept the convention of the colour red as a labelling system that allows us to communicate and make sense of the world. From that point on, trying to convince anyone it is any other colour becomes problematic. People have created a set of these references that they are living by, because our human being-ness still likes predictability and stability that makes us calm in an otherwise world of dynamism and change.

The need for innovative thinking is founded on either problem-solving or exploiting new opportunities. Some inventors focus on improving existing products by looking at the problems of the current known models, whereas others look for new opportunities for functionality or application that can lead to new markets being created. Both are means of improving on the old. For business purposes, the ideas need to be realistic in their application to be useful to society. Products and services ultimately need a market, whether they are fulfilling the demand of an existing need, or creating interest that calls upon the human desire for something different or improved. These three factors of problem-solving, opportunity creation and market demand drive business innovation.

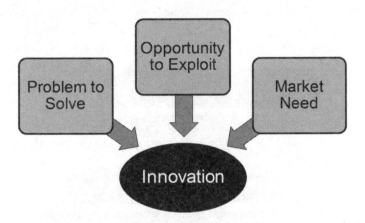

When the problem of not being able to move a desktop computer arose, innovative thinking led to solving this problem through creating a mobile computer device. This is an example of problem-solving. The market already was feeling the limitation of working at the same desk, and the inflexibility of not being able to work from home.

When a programmer started to see how human beings were making decisions based on the manipulation of information, they exploited this opportunity for the computer to follow the same process. They worked out how to manipulate its data in a similar fashion to create a decision-making information management system. The computer started to mimic the human mind, or at least the thinking patterns of the human being modelled. This was exploiting the opportunity of having the data and the known decision process, and making the computer seemingly mimic human reasoning capabilities. A market need was created as it showed how a computer could effectively replace or complement having capable staff.

The challenge is that we humans think very differently primarily based on the complex interweaving combination of our behavioural style, human representational style (communication style), values and beliefs and our unique professional knowledge and expertise. This complex web of possible combinations is what makes each human being so unique, even though they may share some similar traits with another person, such as their behavioural style.

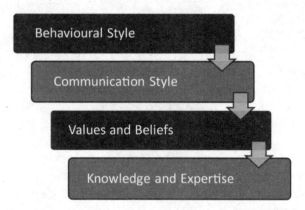

Both the behavioural style, based on a dominating blend of the eight core profile patterns, and the communication style which defines people as being predominantly visual, auditory or kinaesthetic (feelings), are both nature-based traits. This means people are born with them, although they continuously adapt them based on the nurture of life experiences. For example, one may prefer to wear comfortable clothes (kinaesthetic), but if a person were a lawyer their profession would demand a certain dress code to resemble the assumed visual representation of professionalism.

Values and beliefs, which include the fears, doubts and limiting beliefs, as well as individual knowledge and expertise, are all based on our personal life experiences and observations. People were not born with these, individuals developed them and now they occupy most thoughts. For example, an individual may have the perfect behavioural style to succeed in a particular venture, but their beliefs inhibit them from taking any action and therefore they don't get the results. Therefore the most important aspect to getting results is getting thinking right. This is why if an individual wants to change their results, they have to start by changing their thinking:

Thinking + Action = Results

This concept of thinking is quite complex as it blends an idea with an intent, one or more perceived benefits and a conclusion. For a business, the individual's collective innovative thinking, combined with implemented strategy, is what gets results. The misguided actions of one individual can counter the sum of efforts of the remaining team members. This is why it's often said it's best to start with the end in mind, just as products and services should be designed with a particular market in mind. A person can develop the best products in the world, yet if they do not have the market or cannot create one, then they are bound to fail. Too many inventors create amazing products that excite them, but are not attractive to the marketplace. Sometimes it's a timing challenge – the right product, but delivered at the wrong time – or it needs a critical mass of users before it can become effective, like the telephone, facsimile or even applications like Facebook. The trick is not to just create products that are personally liked, but build products that the market needs today or would most likely desire.

The challenges of the biases of human thought and how the brain operates can be overcome through innovative thinking techniques. The key difference with humanistic businesses is that they tend to approach innovation with an emphasis on its impacts on the people involved or the end users in mind, including their environments. It follows the principle that in design work the innovators need to look towards ways of adding value to the users and do it in a way so that the users feel ethically and morally good about what they are doing. Humanistic businesses aim to do the right thing as:

socially responsible interactions are good for business.

Humanistic businesses strive to create value-adding products and services that are designed around the end user. Ideally these will help the user to do things faster, easier, more efficiently and even more ethically. These products and services are benefit-focused, such as clothes that have not used animals in their make-up or testing, or been manufactured in appalling conditions for the workers.

More important is to recognise the need for wider human input in innovative thinking. Business problems or processes can be both difficult and complex. Difficult problems or processes can be broken down into bite-sized chunks to make them simpler to tackle and easier to overcome by an individual. Business process is designed by looking at the functionality of its individual steps and their interrelationship with other elements, in order to define and improve the whole process. Complex problems, however, are more challenging as they call upon a need for differing perspectives, and hence a multiple-person input. They do not break down so easily into simple parts, but are multi-faceted, which calls for different thinking paradigms to overcome them.

Psychologists use a finding and shaping process to look at the constituent parts of a problem, which then leads to an insight into the conditions that caused it in order to find a way to overcome it. Of course, there is never only one solution, but the path to a solution may not be so easily found because of our dominating thinking patterns and our personal reference values and beliefs. Collectively we can work against one another's thinking paradigms to find new thinking approaches or cause a shift in our base thinking·models which changes our perspective enough to be able to see new ways of contemplation. The basis of this thinking to create innovation can be applied to the business model itself, or its systems and processes, and to the products and services, or even a single problem resolution activity. To do this, we look towards perception-challenging techniques that alter the way people look at problems.

The Six Thinking Hats Method

Academic author Dr Edward de Bono developed the 'six thinking hats' model[1] to allow people, especially in a group setting, to become aware of their dominating thinking perspective, and to be able to manipulate their thinking biases to encourage clearer, more effective thinking and drive creative processes.

It works on the principle that we tend to look at things from the same perspective unless prompted to do otherwise. Dr de Bono suggests we imagine a thinking paradigm based on a set of differently coloured hats where each colour represents thinking from a specific perspective. The colours represent statistical, intuitive, pessimism, optimism, creativity and overview thinking models. By associating with a particular colour, you become aware of a specific new perspective.

Expanding on the 'six thinking hats' model, in today's world and from a humanistic standpoint, a purple hat is needed to represent the long-term ecological effect that a decision will have on the purpose and vision of the organisation, the effect on the brand in the marketplace and the overall effect for all stakeholders.

Generally, this 'six thinking hats' technique can be used by an individual who needs to be able to consider different perspectives, or during a group session where the members are assigned different hats to inspire diverse thinking.

The Kipling Questioning Method

Based on the thinking of Rudyard Kipling, this technique involves a set of questions that are proposed and worked through. We are conditioned to answer and respond to questions, so this method drives the perspective of our thinking. The questions are designed to be short, general in their application and direct, and aim to define the problem at hand. The original Kipling 5 Ws[2] comprised:

- **Who** is it about?
- **What** happened?

- **When** did it take place?
- **Where** did it take place?
- **Why** did it happen?

The questions can be extended, using this same principle, and can also be designed around a specific industry or environment. Consider applying the following to a specific problem:

- What is the problem?
- Where is it happening?
- When is it happening?
- When doesn't it happen?
- Why is it happening?
- Why does it not exist?
- Who is involved?
- Who is influencing it?
- What are the boundaries around the problem?
- What are the possible causes?
- How can we replicate it?
- How can it be overcome?
- When will we know it is resolved?

Sometimes defining a problem and its parts well, and identifying when it occurs and when it does not, provides new insight to the key factors and conditions as to when, how and why it is happening. This in turn offers information on the influencing factors that can be eliminated or modified to get to a different result. It focuses on the concept that if a problem's boundaries are identified and then overcome, then there is no problem left, and the opportunity is to find the conditions in which it would exist.

The Toyota Lean Philosophy

The lean method is applied mainly to process improvement, and is aimed at preserving value with less effort. It's based on the work of the Toyota motoring company and derived from the Japanese Toyota

Production System,[3] which provides a philosophy that can be applied using many different quality-based tools.

Its key philosophy is to maintain the flow of a process, while eliminating waste. It aims to break down and analyse each step in the process and seek improvement through focusing firstly on how the process can flow with more ease. It means that at no point in the process should there be an overflow, meaning that if two machines were running, both machines would run not at full capacity, but would match the input and output rates of one another. This avoids any stockpiling in front of any one machine which would cause double handling by having to move the material aside and then back into the process. This method can be used for the ordering of material, maintaining low on-site stock levels and ensuring the most efficient methods of operation.

Its second main aim is to reduce waste that is not limited to scrap materials, but the number of tools, human and machine time, and any aspects that are deemed unnecessary. Consider using one size bolt instead of two. Ordering new bolts would then be cheaper through bulk buying power, the store would only need one compartment, the manufacturing floor would only need one trip for stock refreshing, the number of tools needed would be halved, and there would be no time lost for the operator in changing tools. Moving the most used items closer to the operator and laying out the operation floor will also achieve the least human and machine movement.

Take the example of Dell computers who enjoyed market success based on offering made-to-order-computers for customers. This meant there were no stockpiles of old models as computer chips frequently changed, and the customer was comfortable with the longer delivery times, preferring the customisation value they received, compared to buying an off-the-shelf product. They accepted that a customised machine would take longer to be delivered, and perceived this choice as a personal benefit.

Applying lean thinking is seeking innovation in faster and more effective ways of doing things, with an emphasis on all aspects of waste elimination in material, human movement, stock management and type of equipment. It begins with creating a current value map that defines the process and then, through analysis of lean opportunities, leads to a future value map, often referred to as value stream mapping. The organisation then updates its systems and processes to the new identified way.

The Reverse Paradigm Method

The reverse paradigm method, developed by business leader Todd Hutchison, aims to set out the traditional thinking paradigms and rules, and identify solutions by looking at a process, product or service in their opposite states or conditions. It begins by looking critically at the current status quo and using a 'what if' scenario in assuming it was the wrong way of doing it or impossible to do it that way, and then finding what other different methods could achieve the same result.

For example, if rocket technology were not available for space travel, then the team would consider how else it could have been achieved. In this case, rocket technology is assumed not to be the answer, but it could be more simply a component like the type of fuel used. Geostationary satellites for example stay in place by a thruster propellant that keeps it pointing to the earth, known as station-keeping. The challenge is that this fuel ultimately runs out and causes the satellite to drift and become unusable. Instead of looking at more efficiencies in the station-keeping process by using a particular fuel, this process assumes that the fuel type is not the right solution and looks towards other and opposite methods.

It helps to consider new innovation as it revisits advances in technology to look for new alternatives that avoids the 'we have always done it this way' mentality that may have been traditionally based on the limited technology that was available at the time.

Consider how we came to have lights in a house. It started as a wood fire, then wax candles, then kerosene lanterns, then electricity generated by kinetic energy through water movement, then chemical combustion or nuclear fission and now photovoltaic (solar) and geothermal power methods. Each innovation was led by advances in technology, but the same outcome was light generation.

The process starts with a definition of the current result (the process, product or service) and to define with detail the prevailing assumptions, conventional rules, technology constraints and the emotional drivers that apply today.

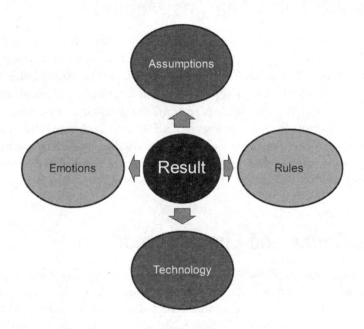

Each of these focal points are then critically analysed to:

- question the assumptions and assume them to be incorrect or no longer valid;
- question the rules and assume they are invalid, limiting or irrelevant;
- question the technology as being old, incomplete or irrelevant with the understanding that they can be replaced with alternatives; and
- question the emotional drivers that represent the traditional market need, buying strategies, user experience, fears and hurts, then to look towards improving or revitalising each.

It works on the principle that what has been done to date was based on historic thinking paradigms, markets and technologies of the past, and calls for questioning the basis or relevance of these and, assuming that they are no longer valid, relevant or now impossible to do, to look at what alternatives could be made to get the same or improved result in today's world.

The Attributes Analysis Method

This decomposition method defines all the attributes of a problem, product or service. It takes a particular object and breaks it down into its constituent parts. Each part then is questioned by asking 'what does this specific element contribute?' and looks towards alternatives, or whether the part is actually needed at all. It follows the same premise of lean production by questioning the usefulness of each activity or item. It looks at the existing positive and negative value it offers to the whole, considering the advantages and disadvantages it presents. The aim is to remove, replace or modify each component part.

The Cause and Effect Method

In 1982, the late Japanese quality advocate, Professor Kauro Ishikawa, developed the fishbone diagram[4] (also referred to as the Ishikawa diagram or cause-and-effect diagram), which is an ideal tool for exploring all the possible causes that may create an unwanted effect. The steps to create the fishbone diagram comprise the following:

1. Define the unwanted effect and write it at the end of the x-axis (the fish's vertebrae);

2. Define each possible grouping of causes that may exist and write them as an angle scale (the fish's ribs). This represents the categories of causes (e.g. equipment, people, processes);

3. Define all possible causes under each category (drawn as lines off the ribs);

4. For each cause, consider 'why does this happen?' This may lead to two or more sub-causes if a particular cause is complex. This should

be repeated until no further causes can be identified, and this identifies the underlying causes, known as the root causes; and

5. Consider any actions that can be undertaken to resolve or remove each cause.

A root cause is the lowest possible level of a cause. The purpose of the fishbone diagram is that if all the causes are examined, including any root causes, and one were able to take action to remove each cause, then the unwanted effect would not exist. The innovation comes from finding methods to eliminate the effect by treating the causes.

The typical categories used for manufacturing-type projects are equipment, process, people, materials, environment and management. For service-based industries, the typical categories are price, promotion, people, processes, place/plant, policies, procedures and product (or service) or, more simply, surroundings, suppliers, systems and skills. If in doubt, consider at least people, process and physical resources. This tool can also be used to identify evidence required in preparation for a legal defence case by collecting all the evidence that the business exercised due diligence in managing each and every cause that related to the legal effect under question.

The Three Principles of Innovation

Innovation and creativity are rarely based on new concepts, but a meeting and mating of ideas to create new combinations. Existing ideas or products brought together in new and surprising ways often grow the sweetest and most rewarding fruit. When individuals draw upon their specialisation for the overall betterment of the organisation and each other, there is a rise in the collective living standards of all. Innovation can provide the sustainable edge to the future of new and old business ventures alike.

There are three primary principles around innovation that humanistic businesses embody to create steady organic growth and therefore sustainability.

Principle 1: Creating productivity with innovation and fun

Tim Brown, CEO of the global design company IDEO, suggests that creating a culture where people have the security to play and not be judged generates greater productivity. He said: 'We need to trust to play and to be creative.' Similarly, Dr Stuart Brown, founder of the National Institute for Play, noted: 'There is good evidence that if you allow employees to engage in something they want to do, [which] is playful, there are better outcomes in terms of productivity and motivation.'

There are many examples of what progressive organisations like Google and LinkedIn are doing to promote productivity through accepting and promoting play activities. At Google employees are paid to play beach volleyball or go bowling. LinkedIn staff have full permission to create play intervals throughout their day. Both organisations give employees time out to follow their passions as they have found that passion is linked to energy that brings on innovative thinking. Play uses the right brain function that can promote more whole brain activity in the workplace. Some of the known benefits of incorporating play into the workplace is that it lowers stress levels, boosts creativity and motivation, opens up new neural pathways in the brain, attracts young talent and increases a positive attitude in staff.

Principle 2: Combining existing ideas to create new products

Dr Teresa Amabile, head of the Entrepreneurial Management unit at Harvard Business School, developed a comprehensive model to explain the three major components required to produce creativity and innovation and therefore new ideas for emerging products and services.

The first component is knowledge, the second is creative thinking and the third is motivation. The theory is that creative thinking alone is not sufficient for producing dynamic new ideas and bringing them to completion, but skill and knowledge, combined with motivation, most certainly can. Market knowledge together with motivation driven by market needs or competitive pressures, coupled with the ability to think outside the box, are perhaps the simplest yet most important qualities for a team to develop. When these three attributes are applied to generating new products and services, an entire new range of offerings can be reviewed and developed, thereby keeping the organisation ahead of prospective developments in their fields.

Principle 3: Explore new connections and applications between two existing products

In his book, *The Medici Effect*,[5] Frans Johansson says: 'We must strike a balance between depth and breadth of knowledge in order to maximise our creative potential.' His suggestion is likened to having a bigger gene pool of knowledge and expertise to generate new and evolving ideas. The greater the knowledge base, the better the development of new connections and applications. According to the triarchic theory of intelligence, devised by US psychologist Robert J. Sternberg,[6] there are three perspectives to generating results, comprising:

- **Synthetic** – the ability to select the relevant from the irrelevant, to combine relevant information in new ways and to combine new information and old information to generate something new;

- **Analytical** – the ability to evaluate one's own ideas, judge whether ideas are useful or not and seek ways to improve; and

- **Practical** – the ability to utilise intellectual skills on a routine basis and influence the buy-in of others.

The heart and soul of Robert Sternberg's message was to develop the skill to combine existing bodies of knowledge and produce something new and useful.

When teams are empowered to innovate and think outside the box and when self-responsibility is infused into every strata of the organisation, innovation teams can be created from every sector of the business to increase the knowledge base and add perspective to creating solutions to new or historical problems, creating ideas that lead to system and process change. Innovation then becomes the life breath of success and sustainability, producing a thriving culture where people become loyal and happy because they find they are valued and their contribution is meaningful.

Happiness is generated by engaging the intellect and the thinking outcomes are used in a way that gives life to new or improved products, services, systems or processes. It makes us feel valued to see our work utilised.

Key Lessons

1. Match business growth cycles with key personal contributors so the growth cycles align with their individual profiles and the team's greatest strengths can be utilised.
2. The business growth cycle begins with innovation, which leads to branding distinction, and then networking of the brand develops into distribution channels that support the sales phase. Delivery and supply creates consistent market penetration, resulting in quality investments and, finally, leads to distribution of assets to stakeholders.
3. A humanistic business collectively engages the spirit of the internal entrepreneur's mind-set so that innovative thinking, coupled with precision strategy, produces the desired results.
4. A humanistic business brings value-adding products to the market that are designed with the end user in mind. It drives products and services to market to produce results faster and easier and remains ethical in all business dealings.
5. A humanistic business aims to do the right thing in the communities they serve. Socially responsible interactions are good for business.
6. Focusing on a problem area often creates more clarity because the de-cluttering process begins, which simplifies the complexity of the problem so that insight is gained.
7. There are three primary principles surrounding humanistic business to create steady organic growth:
   - creating productivity with innovation and fun;
   - combining existing ideas to create new products; and
   - exploring new connections and applications between two existing products.

1. De Bono, E. (1999). *Six Thinking Hats,* Back Bay Books.

2. Kipling, R. (1902). *The Kipling 5 Ws Method.*

3. Lean Enterprise Institute (2008). Lean Lexicon, Lean Enterprise Institute, http://www.lean.org/Common/LexiconTerm.aspx?termid=353, accessed 22 November 2013.

4. Wikipedia (2013). Kauro Ishikawa accessed http://en.wikipedia.org/wiki/Kaoru_Ishikawa, accessed 22 November 2013.

5. Johansson, F. (2006). *The Medici Effect: What Elephants and Epidemics Can Teach Us About Innovation*, Harvard Business Review Press.

6. Sternberg, J. (1984). *Beyond IQ: A Triarchic Theory of Human Intelligence*, Cambridge University Press.

Chapter 6

Developing Self-Leadership

One of the most important elements in creating and sustaining a humanistic business is the investment in human equity and talent development through evolving up-and-coming leaders. New talent evolution and succession follow a natural evolutionary cycle of inter-dependency. Self-leadership is the prerequisite for authentic congruent leadership which wins the trust of the teams and inspires motivation and productivity. Self-leadership is taking ownership of one's thoughts, as well as responsibility for one's actions. Leaders in executive roles of a business have legitimate authority for the organisation and hold the highest possible influence over the business. This said, all team members, whatever their role, must harness their own self-leadership to take control of their life and contribute more effectively to the business in a constructive manner. A humanistic business is one that is aligned to values, purpose and mission, as well as being invested in the wellbeing of all stakeholders, from customers to employees. It is a one-for-all and all-for-one mentality, and each person contributes to the whole experience.

Today's customer is more sophisticated and the competition more fierce than ever before. If organisations are to thrive in such challenging times, they can no longer place profit before people. Often organisations remain invested in a hierarchical, centralised model of leadership where the senior management is isolated from the rest of the organisation preventing them from seeing the organisation as one integrated unit serving in a purposeful way. Without a full and meaningful integration, organisations will continue to operate in silos which will lead to disengagement and inefficiencies. Evolving organisations must turn their focus towards a new business model that creates a new business DNA to adapt to a dynamic world.

Although lower prices and better products are important for a business to remain competitive, they are no longer the competitive edge for customer loyalty. Price and product are fundamental to success, but customer loyalty to the brand is dependent on the experience of their initial and on-going engagement. People want to feel special and cared for and prefer to do business with organisations they like, trust and believe in. Yet they've been bombarded with deceptive, deceitful and unethical marketing for so long that they have become sceptics.

The positive emotional engagement of the end user experience also applies to staff. This is reflected in their own loyalty to the organisation when it is evident they believe in what the organisation stands for, whether it be the board members reflecting the organisation's values in their decision-making, or the follow-on actions of the organisation demonstrating its higher purpose. These have an emotional appeal for everyone involved in the business. Anything less will show through in personal body language, language and attitude. Put simply, genuine authenticity has appeal and can be sensed in many ways.

Humanistic leadership embraces the value of emotional intelligence and people intelligence with an educational commitment to establishing a deep understanding of human nature and the complexity of the different systems of business at play. In fact, one key characteristic of a humanistic business is its culture of career-long learning. The western culture average retail business gives their staff seven hours of training, with no formal plan for on-going professional development commitment. In contrast, the eco-friendly Container Store in the US provides 235 hours of training to their full-time employees in their first year alone, and 160 hours thereafter. The heartbeat of humanistic-based leadership has education at its foundation. Increasing its insights into the importance of people intelligence as well as knowledge of business systems are both seen as vital requirements to improve culture and strengthen the brand energy.

The educational curriculum includes the development of personal self-awareness, analytical, spiritual and emotional intelligence, all of which contribute to the health of organisational relationships.

Humanistic leadership, and the education of its internal stakeholders, creates an overriding higher intelligence and purpose that underpins all organisational activities in the execution and operation of the business. The antiquated way that many organisations still operate their business is based upon analytical thinking, overriding profit concerns and constant fire-fighting. A truly humanistic business is fuelled by its higher purpose and mission, coupled with passionate leadership which eventuates in higher profits and improved culture.

A healthy combination of talent and shared values is the key to successful and long-term professional relationships. This is the basis of the success enjoyed by not-for-profit organisations whose committed teams are usually attracted to them because of this sense of engagement and alignment with the organisation's purpose.

Customers experience the values and culture of an organisation through all contact points, from website information, conversations with staff and interactions with the organisation's frontline team members. Unless staff members believe in what the organisation stands for, they will not be fully committed at an emotional level to do their part in representing the brand. If the well-crafted business strategies of upper level boardroom strategic meetings fail to translate this vision across to the customer, the efforts to create a sustained profitable bottom line and dynamic culture will ultimately fail.

The critical first step in transforming the organisation begins with defining its values and purpose. This is necessary not only to set the moral compass for the business, but also to provide the metrics for measuring its behaviour.

The next step is teaching the fundamentals of leadership throughout the organisation so all internal stakeholders receive similar life skills, aligned values and language. This provides a standard basic knowledge level that enables better understanding and communication.

The Achilles heel that causes organisational vision and mission to fall apart lies within the complex relationship dynamics of the operating teams, which may have individuals with misaligned self-interests. Once incongruence and disconnect occurs between the promoted vision and values and the organisation's practices and actions, the morale of teams falters and segregated silos of power begin to form, destroying a desirable culture and creating disharmony. When this disconnect becomes commonplace in meetings, policies, staff training and management behaviour, the organisation's credibility fails and breeds poor performance. Before the leadership realises it, the organisation is already off course, and sadly they don't know how to steer it back.

There are varying reasons why teams underperform, from poor leadership, poor management, prolonged unresolved historical problems, system dysfunction and even personality conflicts. Usually the root causes boil down to staff disillusionment between what they were told in their job interview and what they experience in their everyday operations. Often the values and mission are not lived and expressed. Staff members witness poor leadership, management dysfunction and lack of information flow on a daily basis and historic problems continue to remain unaddressed, creating a fog of hopelessness.

Often the feedback from teams is that their leaders are not communicating the business's vision and objectives well. When the situation is studied more carefully, it becomes evident that the leaders are not clear about where they are going, so it's not just an unwillingness to communicate, but a lack of knowledge about what to communicate.

Leadership that becomes sustainable begins with individual self-awareness and a commitment from the organisation to invest in its talent. Teams require the knowledge to be able to raise leadership skills, to take emotional responsibility, problem solve, explore different perspectives of a problem, innovate solutions and enter into authentic conversations. The leaders' focus must remain on finding resolutions and innovating new ideas, rather than on positioning for power and personal significance. At the lowest level, staff simply want clarity about their role, task responsibilities and timelines, as well as the support, empowerment and resources they need to execute these.

The end result from a good level of personal investment is that the organisation's products or services not only create better profit margins and it becomes a greater culture to work within, but it can also benefit society as a whole and have the means to contribute in some meaningful way to the community in which they do business.

The speed of technology is such that companies cannot compete endlessly on price, selection or even innovation alone. The best efforts and innovation is generally challenged, beaten or duplicated within a year of a new launch. The ability to capture market share fast is vital, as competitors' equivalent products will only be delayed in entering the market for a short while. These competing products can then cause price wars where the demand increases, but the price reduces and therefore profit is made more on volume.

Innovation, price and delivery are all crucial to the bottom line, but the place where an organisation can capture and hold on to the edge in the market is within the brand distinction. Products can be copied, but the way leadership is engaged in all aspects of the business is hard to replicate as its make-up is often hidden in the intangibility of the culture. The development of employees' talents is the heart of how the customer experiences the brand, product and service. Great customer experience equals sustainable profit. Great customer service is more than a required set of interaction rules laid out in a brief training course on customer service, it's about creating an enthused advocate who truly believes in what the organisation stands for. In the end, your best investment in brand distinction is the commitment to promoting and practicing the organisation's core values and the training and investment in the employees' talents. When an organisation does good for their people, they do good for the business. The profit point is the relationship created between the staff and the customer. This frontline interaction is not easy for your competitors to copy, and is often the overlooked asset to sustainability.

However brilliant your sellable items (products and services) are, the frontline staff and the many touchpoints used by the business which directly engage the customer is where the relationship is made or destroyed. Statistics often show the conversion rate from a single trans-action, not realising that the success starts with a relationship and a transaction may not follow until after several interactions.

In fact, research shows that only 10 per cent of salespeople make more than three contacts, yet 80 per cent of sales are made on the fifth to twelfth contact. While this reflects the old belief that sales is a numbers game, the reality is that, given options, people will not do business with people they do not like and trust. It's less of a numbers game than a relationship game.

This means the salespeople and the support team members need to work in unison. Many organisations seek to resolve difficulties within teams or management that essentially distils down to the dynamics of its own people. Often the separate departments and their managers dig into their respective trenches, planning how to win the unseen battle of wills between the perceived good guys and bad guys within the same departments, teams and behavioural types. All this drama is caused by a lack of leadership skills and an ability to see people as equally needing a positive reaction. The staff and customer interaction must be emotionally positive for a win-win scenario that creates a desire to do work again with each other. As the customer gains similar responses with other staff members, they then come to trust in the brand and not just the individuals. Dealing with the business becomes a repeatable positive interaction. The trust in the individual has been passed to the organisation and brand.

The cost to team and organisation when this frontline is not working is astronomical. Productivity drops and disgruntled employees withhold and clog the flow of information, all of which sabotages productivity.

Humanistic leadership helps to turn the focus from self to service. When individuals do not take responsibility, they enter a team with the view that someone else is to blame for the results of their life and the results of their careers.

The ultimate aim is to achieve a synergy where self becomes intrinsically embedded in the team, and the team becomes represented in the brand. This synergy is the one-for-all mentality, and where the customer and supplier become part of the brand community and, together, contribute to fulfilling a wider purpose in society. Profits can be put into good use in donations, sponsorship and personal contributions to outside causes.

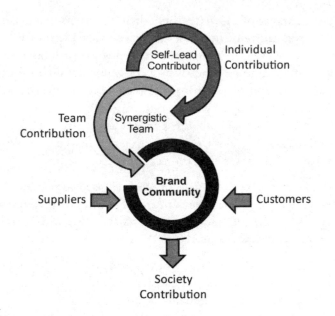

This humanistic model requires an individual to bring their talents to the team, who then works synergistically to serve the customer through the brand, and where the brand community is the culture that attracts the right staff, the right suppliers and the right customers. Through this success comes the ability to be able to generate profit and use it in meaningful ways to improve society.

It also starts with the premise that the individual's self-leadership is centred on doing the right thing, taking a service-based role into making improvements to the environment surrounding them. The consequences of inadequate leadership training and continued victim-mentality thinking are devastating to a humanistic culture, staff retention and the bottom-line profit.

Christine Pearson, Professor of Management at the Thunderbird School of Global Management, and Christine Porath, Assistant Professor of Management at Marshall School of Business at the University of Southern California, have spent much of their careers studying the effects of incivility and a lack of leadership development throughout the ranks of organisations. The consequences of leaving talent under-developed are surprising. Between 1999 and 2005, DaVita Dialysis was under the guidance of a new CEO who believed in operating the organisation from a centre of positive values, the very heart of humanistic business. In a six-year period the company went from a quarter-million in capitalisation to more than five billion by installing a management leadership team committed to positive values and positive attitudes, with staff turnover dropping by a whopping 50 per cent, which allowed the talent to be retained and added more value to the team. The huge cost in staff turnover alone is often underestimated or unknown by organisations, not to mention the cost of recruitment.

In her book *The Cost of Bad Behaviour*,[1] Porath focuses on Cisco Systems and discovered that if even one per cent of staff corrupted a team with incivility and a lack of leadership, the cost of lost productivity and employees leaving was close to US$12 million a year.

There is a high cost to the bottom line of companies who are not engaged in talent management. It may be costly to train staff, but it has proven to be more costly if you don't. Equally, there is often a risk of losing them once you have trained them, but what if you don't train them and they stay? The trick is to develop them towards their peak performance, and at the same time create the environment that will retain them.

According to Porath, the cost to employers of finding and training a suitable replacement with no guarantees that the new employee will stay any longer than the last, is 1.5 times to 2.5 times an employee's annual salary. The hidden financial impact is enormous and often drives a business into the ground.

If management believes the cost of staff development is too high, try reflecting on the cost of doing nothing. The global Project Management Institute undertook a study[2] that showed that for every US$1 billion spent on projects, US$135 million was unrecoverable waste. They concluded that there were three core attributes to the high-performing organisations that were wasting 14 times less than those low performers: a focus on talent management; support of standardisation (methodology); and a drive to have strategic alignment. Examining these it shows that the high performers were following a strategy, that their systems and processes guided good behaviour and that the investment in building and retaining talent was critical. The strategy gives clarity to the team, the processes support the right practices and it is then the self-led individuals who, working together synergistically, get the results.

For true empowerment of an employee, the leadership must consider the seven key attributes. Firstly, the person needs to be aligned to the organisation's purpose, values and strategy. They need the resources and management support to do their job effectively. They must understand their role and its authority and the responsibilities it brings. They must act with self-leadership so that they take self-accountable actions and strive to do their best in the interests of the business and its key stakeholders, and they must continue to develop and refine their knowledge and expertise (talent management).

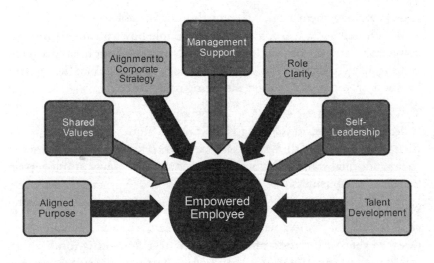

People genuinely desire to do a good job when they enter an organisation. Rarely do new team members intentionally desire to decrease the effectiveness of an existing team. People often simply lack the education of how to move beyond the emotional conditioning of their past and gain understanding between themselves and other team members. They don't have the knowledge, life skills or training, and within a short time become entrenched into the culture. The old-time employees often resist management's efforts for change, suggesting 'we have seen it attempted before'. What they often don't realise is that their own inactions, lack of support and negatively expressed remarks are the reason why the change is resisted or it fails, only so they can say 'I told you so'. It becomes a self-fulfilling prophecy.

The objective of functioning teams is to harvest the genius that is hidden in the diversity of different perspectives and to drive those differences towards innovation and productivity. Complexity, compared with complication, requires a different perspective for it to be overcome. It needs a team working together to provide resolve and to collectively bring ideas into being. For example, the individual with the most technical behavioural style acts to improve on existing processes, like the software developer who constantly looks to improve the functionality of the software.

It is the management team's responsibility to establish understanding of the diversity of a team, and to train people how to think, problem solve, respect and work with the diversity that keeps a business reinventing itself in ways that it does not age and die. This keeps the business on top of the market, surviving and thriving.

Team members need education and support in keeping a great attitude, utilising and developing their talents, finding ways to express their own talents within the team context, taking responsibility for their emotional states and contributing in positive ways for the overall benefit of the business.

Without the development of these fundamental humanistic leadership skills across all the teams, the separate team choices generally boil down to the self-interests of their line managers working in isolation (often with positive intent for their own department's results).

We must recognise as leaders that each person lives from a mind-set that has a very different story based on their own past experiences and they see their world through a different set of filters, which colours their world differently. It is vital for leaders to understand these differences so the feelings can be addressed, accountability can be maintained and empathy developed. Again, it is the differences in values that make the greater divide.

A further consequence of not teaching the skills of humanistic leadership is that individuals become increasingly disconnected, and defensive. Their behavioural style will be expressed outwardly or silently through passive aggressive behaviour.

When management silently ignores these dynamics, silos of power form within teams that work against the overall objective of team cohesion. The end result of this type of team dynamics is a brutal blow to building a culture where people desire to come to work and remain productive. Without the establishment of empowered humanistic leadership within all the ranks, an organisation cannot have a high level of productivity, which in turn means repressed profit.

In lean economic times an organisation that sustains its profit margins will heal this gaping wound within itself and survive the rising costs of doing business. The answer is quite simply that business success is a people game, and to survive we have to invest in humanistic leadership development so the game can be played more effectively.

The humanistic business pillar that humanistic leadership serves is based on people's desire to do business with people who act with integrity. This is the basis for the principle that people strive for repeatable positive experiences. Likeability and trust can only be established through people understanding people, personal self-leadership and individual accountability with emotional self-management. As staff embrace the principles that empower them in every context of their lives, incivility lessens dramatically, the culture improves and staff retention becomes natural. The internal culture improvement energises brand energy, creates market interest and leads to repeat customer loyalty. When organisations do good by their stakeholders, it is good for business.

There exist six guiding principles for managers to lead the establishment of self-leadership and a supportive culture.

Take responsibility

The first principle is to introduce the idea that people are responsible for their own emotional responses. Organisations must educate their teams to realise that no one is a victim, that individuals do have a choice over their emotional responses and can take responsibility for the results that their choices lead to.

Previous thinking has produced certain results in a person's life which has led to certain choices made with the information and resources available at that time. The events, within themselves, are neutral, but each person ascribes a positive or negative interpretation to the meaning behind them. This first principle to realise is that the past results are not necessarily a reflection of future results.

Organisations have to bring together diverse personalities from many walks of life, age groups, ethnic backgrounds, religions, educational levels, ancestral influences and perceptual differences. Leadership comes from guiding all these people to act professionally, to work as a synergistic team and to drive a service or product out to market with profit-exploding potential. It is a fantasy for a leader to think it happens naturally. If organisations desire sustainable change, increased profit margins and unbeatable branding, then a deeper skill set of leadership must be introduced to develop positive attitudes and perspectives that are conducive to the business's success. Personal accountability, emotional management and people intelligence must be introduced from the board members down to the point where staff engages the customer.

Build respect

The second principle is the need to establish and build respect and trust. This can be achieved through four key steps, described below, that will create a culture within your team where people desire to belong.

1. Establish a clear, concise and values-driven strategy that provides a clear direction, and communicate it to every member of the team. To engage buy-in from staff, it's important that each team member understands how their individual responsibilities fit into the achievement of the overall team objective. Clarity is king. The second fundamental human need, as identified by Abraham Maslow, is a sense of belonging or being part of a tribe. Make it clear that every staff member's contribution is a vital component in the accomplishment of the team's desired objective, and you will begin to instil a sense of purpose. People want to feel they are an important part of the team's overall objective and that what they do, both personally

and collectively, matters. They want to feel they are making a purposeful contribution and that what they do daily is valued.

2. Listen to others and be proactive as it helps to build respect when a person knows their voice has been heard and acknowledged. Know what the team members require, what their dreams are and what their frustrations are. It's vital to understand what is working well and what is not. Remember, team members will see things that management may miss and will have new, innovative ideas for solving historical problems. Learn to listen more and pontificate less.

3. Strive to always be truthful. It only takes once for a leader to be caught in a lie to have the trust fall apart and the respect vanish. Always tell them the truth, as they deserve to know the information that impacts them. The more transparency that a leader shows, the greater the trust and respect that will build in teams. Be vulnerable yet powerful. Vulnerability comes from transparency. Strength can exist side by side with vulnerability by having the courage to innovate ideas and resolve problems, while realising your strengths and weaknesses equally. Tell the truth, live by your word and respect and trust will be built.

4. Include team members in what is happening in the department and give them a role of intrepreneur or staff innovator. Train staff how to think, innovate and problem solve, allowing time for brainstorming sessions to tackle historical problems with systematic thinking to bring innovative ideas to management for approval and implementation. This one element alone creates strong team cohesion and brings solutions, ideas and new systems to the focus of management, while providing staff with a voice to improve conditions within their work environments.

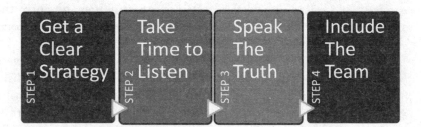

Remember the humanistic business pillar that people strive to create repeatable positive experiences, and these form positive relationships acting as a primary key to success. Without integrity there can be no trust because people desire to maintain repeatable positive experiences in their dealings with others. Without integrity this pillar crumbles.

Establish integrity

The third principle is to establish integrity as an organisational value to be represented in the behaviour of the management and every stakeholder. Integrity must also be reflected in all policies as well as in the mission statement of the organisation. The most important element will be how well integrity is demonstrated on a day-by-day operational basis.

In a recent post[3] on '*10 Mistakes Leaders Should Avoid at All Costs*' on Michael Hyatt's Intentional Leadership blog, Enrique Fiallo commented on the importance of integrity in leadership: 'There are many things you can lack and still steer clear of danger. Integrity isn't one of them. Establish a set of sound ethics policies, integrate them into all business processes, communicate them broadly to all employees, and make clear that you will not tolerate any deviation from any of them. Then live by them.'

The one aspect of this great statement that many leaders miss is 'live by them'. And they don't walk their talk. You cannot establish trust, respect and integrity without demonstrating it in real-life workplace scenarios. The quickest way to destroy credibility as a leader is through inconsistent actions with what has been voiced or agreed. These more subtle soft skills are actually the backbone and life breath of authentic humanistic leadership. It is and will forever be how self-leadership is demonstrated seamlessly in leadership behaviours. A leader cannot demand of someone else what they do not do within their own behaviours and expect people to trust, respect and follow them.

Develop empathy

Empathy is recognising the challenges in the situation, but not dropping down into sympathy. It's the ability to listen to another and be aware of how their perception has impacted their feelings. This does not mean that there is an agreement with how they perceive the world. Stories that people are creating inside their heads are different from person to person, and thereby the colour of realities becomes diverse. Empathy simply means to strive to understand another's model of the world, as the stories in people's heads impact the flood of emotions that govern and drive their behaviour. The better a person can understand others, the better they can motivate and help individual team members to optimise their performance.

The quality of empathy dovetails into the quality of respect and trust, because without empathy, there will be little or no trust and respect maintained or established. The act of empathy is one of the pillars of maintaining and establishing trust and respect. If a person does not feel understood or listened to, one can say goodbye to trust and respect.

Often a manager will sit with a troubled team member, only half engaged, with their focus divided between the staff member in front of them and the urgent report that is due. This is not genuine empathy when you are not fully engaged. Humanistic leadership displays boundaries, authenticity, trust and respect. The actions that demonstrate these qualities are listening, not being judgmental, understanding another person's circumstances and empathy. Empathy takes time in your daily calendar, but here are a few of the benefits of practicing empathy in leadership.

- All relationship success is based on the strengthening of relationships. Empathy helps build the trust required in all lasting relationships and improves team cohesion.

- With a better understanding of staff members, the leader will find it easier to come up with strategies to help a struggling or underperforming person resolve their difficulties and contribute to their team with greater congruency. When people feel cared for and respected, they thrive and become loyal members of the team, excelling way beyond their past performance and emerging as enthused advocates of the brand. When staff are criticised and demeaned, they become hostile or passive aggressive.

- Most importantly, empathy establishes emotional safety. People do not need to be perfect, but they do require the opportunity to improve and grow. It is the leader's responsibility to care for and help empower the team members to excel and improve their thinking, lives and job performance. Practicing empathy as part of leadership responsibilities gains respect and loyalty from staff. The micro culture within individual teams will then be powered by the goodwill to truly understand others.

Increase people intelligence

The fifth principle in establishing humanistic leadership is to increase your people intelligence. So little understanding of people is actually gained from the conversations held or the words spoken to one another that give insights into thinking paradigms, and beliefs. The definition of people intelligence is the ability to read non-verbal cues from one another, understand the assumptions underneath the language choices that another person makes and to determine the thinking strategies being used.

Language symbolises and directs our thinking, and thinking builds emotional states which drive our behaviour. To understand people, motivate people and determine the inherent potential of a person's actions, simply listen to their language choices and watch their body language. As a leader develops this knowledge of reading unconscious non-verbal cues of body language and the presuppositions inherent in another's language choices, they can begin to gain powerful insights into the inner world of the people in their respective teams, so that better communication can be achieved. Having the skill to navigate through the complexities of human relationships is one that will set an organisation's leadership development apart from the rest.

Empower your staff

The sixth principle of humanistic leadership is based on the fact that doing good is good for business. Empowering staff to come up with new ways of resolving difficulties in their teams not only benefits the team and the organisation, but also every aspect of the staff members' lives, further endearing the staff to you. When an organisation respects and cares for the wellbeing of their staff, it secures their success.

So, this sixth and final principle is about creating an organisation so that it embeds 'systems thinking', a method which looks at problems in a holistic way in order to find lasting and workable solutions. The father of systems thinking is Peter Senge, founding chair of the Society for Organizational Learning, which focuses upon decentralising the role of leadership in organisations and enhancing the ability for all people to work productively towards common goals.

Systems thinking is about expanding management's vision to divert from quick short-term solutions that achieve short-term results, but with little consideration for the long-term consequences. Often management's decisions are focused upon the part, rather than the whole, of a very complex system. When the focus is upon the long-term effects, more appropriate consideration can be given to the impact on the system. Short-term solutions often produce significant long-term negative consequences. For example, cutting back on staff development training may save money in the short run, but a lack of investment in talent will lower morale, lessen productivity, increase staff turnover and negatively impact on the brand energy and the interface between staff and customers. As a result, sales drop, the brand is compromised, the culture becomes toxic and profits drop long term.

An organisation may minimise funds for research and create huge savings in the short term, but end up losing its innovative edge in the market, giving competitors the opportunity to gain market share.

When an organisation fails to incorporate and embrace systems thinking, the overall impact on culture, morale, productivity and profit has dire consequences on its sustainability. An organisation cannot maintain momentum with an immediate 'put-out-the-fire' decision focus, which ultimately results in negative consequences further down the track.

The solution is simple: focus on the decentralisation of leadership and invest in people development with a deeper understanding of systems dynamics, innovation and solution generation. This approach will protect an organisation from victim-mentality thinking and the wasted energy used in fault-finding and witch-hunting the person or department responsible for why things aren't working.

The solution is always closer than many might think. When organisations stop blaming and wasting time and energy and begin embracing the power of humanistic leadership by starting to think differently, focusing on the direction ahead, honouring humanity in business and teaching leadership throughout every strata of the organisation, they reach a position of empowerment.

When organisations fail to establish an understanding of their complex systems diversity, train people how to think, problem solve, take responsibility, respect and welcome each other's differences, then they will be left with few options but to tread water, just surviving in business. This is the difference between survive and the potential to thrive.

Without the human element being set right up front, which becomes the foundation for growth, a business cannot have high sustainable productivity and create long-term profits. For a humanistic business to succeed, it requires each individual to work hard and to do their very best, and for management to support and nurture its talents. All team members must recognise the need for the organisation to grow and maintain the cash flow that allows it to exist and continue.

The foundation of a humanistic approach is to go beyond one's self-interests, with a focus on serving others to one's best abilities, where the ultimate reward is in creating a meaningful and enjoyable work environment that is sustaining and able to provide jobs and do responsible work for society. It really comes down to creating a tribe for the purpose of service and communion with fellow human beings so that we may live more harmoniously.

Once self-leadership is attained, and the team members are working in their self-assured state as self-accountable people, there is a need to have a voice, to speak at those vital conversation times, and be able to do that in an open, honest and respectful way. Humanistic businesses aim to support authentic conversations within their teams.

Key Lessons

1. Empowered staff empower the profit centre where customer meets staff.
2. Enthused advocates energise market interest.
3. Ensuring that values and purpose are humanistic in nature gains the emotional buy-in of stakeholders.
4. Turning a drive for profit into service of the stakeholders can lead to sustainable profit.
5. Self-leadership contributes to team synergy. Team synergy builds brand energy, contributing to the communities they serve.
6. When the organisation is aligned with the seven principles of humanistic business they create an environment for the empowerment of staff.
7. People prefer to do business with those who act with integrity.
8. Build trust and respect through the four key steps to creating a great culture.
9. To sustain trust and respect you must have empathy.
10. Increase people intelligence to resolve differences and build effective communication between team members.
11. Systems thinking awakens the innovation of the entrepreneurial spirit in staff.
12. Leadership changes culture through the adoption of the principles in all strata of the organisation.

[1] Pearson, C., Porath, C. (2009). *The Cost of Bad Behaviour: How Incivility is Damaging Your Business and What To Do About It*, Portfolio Hardcover.

[2] PMI (2013). *Pulse of the Profession*, Project Management Institute.

[3] http://michaelhyatt.com/10-mistakes-leaders-should-avoid-at-all-costs.html

Chapter 7

Enabling Authentic Conversations

OVERVIEW

- The quality of our conversations translates to the quality of our relationships.
- Authentic conversations are an essential pillar for building powerfully productive teams.
- Powerful conversations can shift a person's destiny and empower a team to action.
- The importance of the conversation is critical to a thriving culture and the development of humanistic business.

If relationships are at the heart of humanistic businesses, then the quality of our relationships is directly related to the quality of the conversations within those engaging moments. Conversations that build a bridge between different perspectives, so that mutual understanding is achieved and solutions are reached, are critical in any culture. The leadership skill of authentic conversations is the foundation for each of the sections of the humanistic model because it's the source of how differences are resolved, understanding is reached, methodologies are enacted and productivity is preserved among teams.

The key element to establishing and sustaining great working relationships is in the art of communication. Our achievements in business and our careers are based largely upon how successful we've been in establishing productive relationships, and on our likeability and the trust we engender in others.

Organisations can sustain themselves through difficult economic times with a solid loyal team. During the global financial crisis many businesses lost income or went bankrupt. One German car company experienced a 20 per cent loss in revenue. They had few options, but being a family-owned business that cared about their staff and their families, they approached the staff with two options. The management had the choice of either laying off 20 per cent of their personnel or for all the staff to accept a voluntary reduction in their salaries by 20 per cent. The staff opted for the latter and voluntarily reduced their salaries to ride out the storm. The intellectual and experiential wealth of long-term employees was saved and the teams came together to rebuild their company's 20 per cent loss. The company once again secured their reputation by preserving positive relationships, which was key to their success. This creative solution began with an authentic dialogue between management and staff.

Authentic conversations can be managed as a system that provides structure to often difficult communications between vendors, team members and other stakeholders. The system offers an outline to follow while diffusing the emotional impact of difficult conversations. In short, an authentic conversation keeps a set of boundaries around the content of a conversation. It calls for openness, frankness, trust, respect and, most of all, is underpinned with the higher purpose of mutual understanding. This allows everyone to strive for mutual gains that are in the best interests of a wider group. The authentic conversation is free of sarcasm, blame, victim mentality and ridicule, and instead is enriched by a genuine desire to see things from the other party's perspective, to avoid interpreting any feedback as criticism and to truly listen. It is a two-way dialogue with the purpose of serving the needs of all parties in a positive and constructive manner.

An authentic conversation is an essential pillar to creating powerfully productive teams and establishing an emotionally safe culture. Organisations cannot afford the damaging effects of miscommunication to fester among its ranks, which can then grow into bigger problems because there is no forum to hold a conversation that could disperse the fear.

This one element of our lives is where most leaders, and those committed to success, lose their footing. In order to successfully master the art of relationships and motivating teams, we require new tools, new strategies and a commitment to our leadership.

For many of us, relationships have been the uncharted territory where we are left without a compass or map to find our way to reach the destination of effectiveness, understanding, contentment and happiness and a positive working culture. It's therefore unreasonable to expect that a diverse group of employees can come together and magically produce great service, optimal efficiency and a thriving, healthy culture without the necessary skills.

The principal competency of relationship skills rests upon the ability to create conversations that matter, are results-oriented, first-person accountable and which produce solutions. This one competency underpins all relationships and supports a thriving culture. The hallmark of a great leader is the ability to win the trust and loyalty of the teams they lead. Motivation of a team is dependent on whether trust and respect has been established by the leaders.

A powerful conversation can shift a person's destiny and empower a team to action. Imagine the results that a team could achieve if they had mastered a strategy to hold authentic conversations steeped in the intention to build bridges between differences. When conversations become open and transparent, the productivity created makes a world of difference.

When team members mend relationships through self-leadership and resolve issues of miscommunication, the culture evolves. Every conversation that is held reflects who we have become. When conversations are in alignment with our deepest-set values, those values are reflected in the conversations and relationships thrive, and the team leadership matures.

The depth of ability to hold such a conversation will be equal to the depth to which the leadership has matured. One is in direct measure to the other, and without the authentic conversation the quality of any relationship will slowly deteriorate and leadership qualities will remain weak.

The hidden destructive pattern that often goes unrecognised is the silent message that is being sent, which results from an inability and lack of courage to step forward and hold a conversation that is authentic. Not only does this result in lower self-esteem, but resentment for the other person builds.

When conversational withholding occurs in management and team dynamics, there is no quicker way to destroy respect and trust among a team than for team members to remain inauthentic.

It's important to recognise how powerful conversations can be when people show up fully present, honest, accountable and authentic. A conversation can change a nation. It can also offer clarity, remedy miscommunication and empower the position to heal a relationship. Unfortunately, in the absence of information, people make up stories and these are rarely positive. Individuals tend to think the worst when information is withheld. In contrast, people can move mountains of resistance in a single authentic conversation.

The importance of these types of conversations is critical to a thriving culture and the development of a humanistic business. To learn the art of authentic conversations, consider the following tips and suggestions.

- **Tip #1** Make an investment in personal self-leadership by identifying and operating from a set of personal values, fuelled by the courage to understand and respect the diversity of other people.

- **Tip #2** Utilise one pointed focus of attention to establish trust with the inner intention of building bridges between different points of view and opposing points of view, so that understanding and empathy can be reached.

- **Tip #3** Learn to listen, reflect, pause and deliberate by taking multiple perceptual positions so the topic of discussion can be reviewed from different points of view. People act with positive intent, which means that all their actions are based on having some benefit. Become less judgmental and start looking at their perspective from an empathetic viewpoint that is focused on motivating interests.

- **Tip #4** Build a physiological rapport with the other person. Set a mutually desired goal that is agreed by both parties before the conversation begins. Have an overall outcome for the conversation that is mutually agreed in order to manage the risk of the conversation digressing.

- **Tip #5** Have the attitude that right now is the only moment of power to evolve as a leader. It's only in this next conversation that your leadership evolution can change.

- **Tip #6** Remember to breathe. Breathe through the nose and exhale through the mouth. This type of breathing actually has a biological effect on the body. The more you breathe in this pattern, the more you can slow the heart rate down and move away from the emotions of fight or flight to a more calmed state. The objective is to move from an immediate response triggered through the limbic system in the brain to the frontal lobe region of the brain where we access our higher reasoning abilities.

By following the above tips individuals can begin to take greater emotional responsibility and gain the courage to hold the conversations that matter. In addition, there are some basic beliefs that can guide us. After years of research and experience on the subject of relationships, the following perspectives were found to be most useful in guiding authentic conversations. These perspectives are neither true nor false, but simply extraordinarily useful in building self-awareness, self-leadership and navigating through the diversity and differences between people.

1. The map is not the territory

Our reality is a construction. Any person's view of reality is therefore not reality, but is the best thing they've been able to create for themselves as an interpretation of the current circumstances based upon their collective memories, filters, beliefs, values and accumulative experiences. What is occurring around each person daily is passed through the learnings of the past. If a situation triggers deep unresolved emotional states then people become more distorted in their perspective and behaviour. As individuals look at life through different lenses they respond to what they're making up rather than what actually may be. Individual maps of reality are not reality, only an interpretation of reality. To self-lead means to question reality and the initial emotional responses and become curious about how many new ways reality can be viewed so that action can be generated more through choice rather than reactive emotions.

2. Relationships are mirrors in which individuals can see the deepest subconscious patterns of ourselves

The heart of self-leadership is to become aware of the patterns we have yet to see within ourselves. The repeating emotional patterns of relationships are windows into our unconscious patterns and responses thereby becoming the laboratory in which self-discovery is made. This one statement is often a bitter pill to swallow as the nature of the ego is to project blame on to another for why we feel the way we do, or why we're not happy, or why our life or career is not working. The constant in the equation of any person's relationship history is themselves, which means we can self-sabotage from this conditioning. Work or intimate relationships can trigger fear or doubt, and disempowering beliefs about self-worth will surface with a vengeance.

Relationships reflect back the deepest emotional patterns and reveal the unconscious blueprint for future relationships. Each person has programmed themselves and their responses. However, they hold the ability to recondition themselves for the better as well.

3. Relationships are meant to evoke our deepest wounds so people have an opportunity to heal

Relationships are a vehicle for leadership growth by providing insights into core behaviour patterns. Relationships mirror back to each person unseen patterns and bring them to consciousness, providing an option to change. The first step to self-leadership is self-awareness as this is the foundation of all leadership development. If leaders desire to fully step into power, to live congruently, then the enormous energy drain of fear and projection that occurs in relationships must stop. The way forward is to take full responsibility for what has been co-created with others and choose to make it different. Relationships will reveal where personal leadership work requires to be focused.

4. The power of empathy in the conversation

The use of empathy within the conversation is key. When another's behaviour is experienced as being unprofessional or aggressive, the questions that will help turn the attention away from a flight or fight response, to a leadership response are as follows:

1. What emotion must be driving them to act the way they are right now?

2. What must they be feeling?

3. How has my interaction with them contributed to the response?

4. What benefit or positive gain could this behaviour be bringing to them?

5. What do I need to ask or say to bring us to a mutual understanding?

Bad behaviour is generally a manifestation of unexpressed fear. People often don't feel acknowledged, seen or important enough and often have a sense of unworthiness or lack confidence. Whatever the trigger, people can choose what outcome is desired for the relationship and base the response to their communication upon that outcome.

There will be times when a person will be so emotionally reactive that a conversation will not be possible. Postpone the conversation to another time in the near future so the conversation can be productive. Remember their reaction has generally more to do with the fear and doubt they are feeling and the story and meaning they have constructed.

People generally respond to the image of what they have made up about a person or situation, rather than the actual reality. The solution is more open communication, and clarifying positions because other people just may be doing their best to do the right thing. Avoid taking reactive responses from others personally, adhere to self-leadership skills and practice empathy. Leaders are required to be the most flexible ones within the system of their relationships and build the muscle of self-leadership. Draw boundaries, and hold the authentic conversation with a true intent to support and nurture one another, while recognising that accountability for one's actions is vital to win the trust and respect of others.

5. Every behaviour is motivated by a positive intention

People make the best choices they can with the resources they have available. Often people's resources are so low that their behaviour reflects their inability to cope with even small stress factors on the job or in their personal lives. Their past could have been riddled with trauma that remains unresolved. They may have a horrible stressful home life that haunts them throughout the day. They may be living in deep fear that remains unresolved as they attempt to cope with the work stresses. What happens elsewhere in life has an influence on other aspects of life. Home life has a roll-on effect on work life.

People can become less judgmental of others when they realise that people act with positive intent in that they are getting some benefit from their actions. Lying may have the benefit of not getting into trouble or avoiding an argument. Or they may not have realised that they had other options, so their actions were based on not recognising their resources and choices. Other times there may be secondary gains, where they have an intent to express one behaviour, but may have some unconscious or even conscious benefits in maintaining the bad behaviour. For example, a smoker may genuinely want to stop smoking for health benefits, but they enjoy the social interaction of going outside for a smoke break, hence they don't want to lose the benefit of being part of the team.

Even though some actions may be based on misaligned values or false beliefs, people still act for some positive purpose inside themselves. Often it just takes understanding and conversations to make them aware of their options, resources and the consequence of their actions in a supportive manner. Hold an authentic conversation with them and help them find the resources they need, as well as providing tools and skills to help them become a more useful member of the team.

6. All outcomes are achievements; there is only feedback

Living is learning and life is constantly teaching us. There are no failures in people's actions or relationships, only feedback that is an accurate reflection of where they are in their leadership development journey.

Mistakes are part of human nature, in fact they tell us what works and what does not, hence why they are learning opportunities. The trick is to actually learn from them to avoid repeating them and to evolve through experiences and observations. Often it appears that when individuals don't learn from their experiences, they repeat the circumstances until they get the insight to evolve.

Take the learning and add to the ability to reflect and grow from each relationship and conversation one engages in. If there remains unfinished conversations between two people the leader requires to prepare and practice the intent, tips and system for authentic conversations and discover whether there exists a willingness to hold the conversation in order to gain clarity and establish a productive way forward. If the other party is unwilling, establish personal willingness and intention to resolve the issue and leave the door open for the conversation at some point in the future.

7. Flexibility is a hallmark of leadership

Flexibility is the key ingredient for success, whether it is flexibility of perception, behaviour or thinking. The more flexible an individual is the more innovative and creative they will be. There are always multiple ways of viewing a situation and it is based upon the perspective that is taken that will allow a person to see the situation differently.

To improve self-leadership, view situations from multiple perspectives to increase flexibility and innovation. People possess the capacity to experience broader understanding and therefore see beyond the constraints of rigid thinking and narrow opinionated conclusions without objectivity. If an individual truly desires to get fast and effective results then this one quality in the leadership toolbox will make a huge difference.

Take the example of input being received through the five senses. Like a computer, this is simply data being received. It's like light coming into the eyes, through the pupil and lens and on to the retina. At that stage it is simply an array of contrasts of light intensity and colour hues, and it takes the brain to interpret this data into information. When one takes that information and gives it meaning, they are creating knowledge. The first time a person gains knowledge about a topic, they cannot explain whether the experience was good or bad, having only had the one experience. Wisdom can only come with experience, as it is only when individuals have had enough experiences that they can gain multiple insights because the knowledge has sufficient depth and breadth.

A leader tends to gain flexibility over time, as they will then have enough diverse knowledge to better understand and evaluate the plethora of options and outcomes that are available. In this way, they come to be less stressed and more adaptable. Of course, there is always the opposite situation where people become less flexible and start resisting change, but this is only to their disadvantage.

The famous Chinese Shaolin Temple makes a good example of this. Shaolin effectively means 'young forest', which shows that in a raging storm, the young tree bends and sways and survives, yet the strong, unbending aged tree fights, breaks and is destroyed. Flexibility is the key to survival.

8. Respect each person's model of the world

Each person deserves respect and honour. Human beings are a complex system of memories, beliefs and values that are often reflected in the use of language, body language and modelling of ancestral patterns and influences. Each individual carries a mountain of personal evidence that their way of interpreting reality is true. Even features in a person's face depict what parts of the brain they have been dominantly using, and this can be used by therapists to indicate past trauma or the key attributes of that person's thinking style.

Based upon individual observations and experiences, the world and circumstances are seen quite differently by each individual. Behavioural profiling has proven that each of us can be easily annoyed by people who are the opposite style, and it takes an understanding of each behavioural style and how they interact to be able to recognise how they work together. Many people think that the conflicts they are experiencing are personality-based, when in fact they are behavioural differences. Take the example of the out-of-the-box creative thinker who is trying to paint a picture of the ultimate situation, but keeps getting interpreted by the detailed thinker who wants to bring it back to reality (in their mind) of what is the next step. They genuinely will annoy one another. However, if they work together, the creative thinker will be able to explain their end vision uninterrupted and then hand over to the details person who can then explain the next transition stage that points the team in the same direction as the vision. The reality is they come to a better result when they work together, and they actually need each other without often realising it.

The quickest way to improve relationship abilities is to honour the differences and respect each person's model of the world without condemnation, choosing rather to build a bridge to mutual understanding between the differences.

> 'You cannot make a decision about anything accurately unless you take a minimum of at least three perceptual positions.'
>
> Gregory Bateson, author, anthropologist, linguist,
> social scientist and cyberneticist

To enhance multiple perspective viewpoints when faced with difficult relationship scenarios, especially where emotional reactions are highly charged, the key is to align to the leadership objectives and ask the following questions of oneself to increase flexibility, empathy generation and perspective:

1. How am I interpreting this situation and am I right?

2. If I am not right, what options would I be considering?

3. Are my assumptions incorrect?

4. What are the emotions driving this situation?

5. What are the emotions that are likely driving the other person's response?

6. How have I contributed to this problem?

7. How many ways can I look at this that would give me another meaning and experience?

8. What lessons may I be missing in this experience?

The Outline and Attitude for the Authentic Conversation

The outline for the authentic conversation gives structure to the steps of practicing conversations that matter. The true purpose of all relationships is to establish trust and stronger relationships because people desire to associate with people they feel safe with and trust. To hold authentic conversations, follow the principles and methodologies described below. Even the most challenging conversations can become a leadership-building opportunity for all parties concerned. Here are some thoughts to consider before the conversation begins:

1. **You are responsible for your own feelings**. The other person does not make you feel anything because you hold the power to give their communication the meaning you choose. When we respond badly to another person's words or actions, it is more about us than them. Sometimes people trigger emotions that connect us to past events that have nothing to do with the person we are conversing with; rather they have come to represent the same unresolved event from our past.

2. **The other person must see the situation differently** from you because they have a different set of experiences that would force

them to do this. Difference and diversity is essential to life. It most often leads to growth as different perspectives can influence thinking and help us to see through our own limiting beliefs. Research is showing that difficult problems can be resolved by one person, but complex problems need a team of diverse-thinking people. We've found that it also links to bringing together people with differing behavioural styles.

3. **You only have to decide what your outcome is** for the conversation and act in a way that your outcome can be achieved, keeping focused upon the outcome throughout the conversation. We are driven by clarity, and purposeful conversation, respects and values. Hence quality conversations tend to be purposeful and offer an opportunity for insight, solutions or clarifications.

4. **Respect the differences** between you and the other person and keep your own personal emotional control. When we allow emotions to take control, we override our logical brain and we often say hurtful, inappropriate and inaccurate statements that we later regret. Self-leadership embeds emotional control. This means knowing when to pull back, when to not continue and when to keep opinions to ourselves.

5. **Now is your only moment of power** to hold the authentic conversation and evolve yourself. The next conversation can begin a new habit that leads to tremendous self-esteem and leadership development. It is never too late to change. The opportunity to take control is in the now.

The following steps guide authentic conversations:

Step 1

Subtly match or mirror the body positioning of the speaker to create an unconscious rapport. Psychologist Albert Mehrabian[1] found that a person's likeability was 55 per cent based on their body language. One can also do the same with speech, by speaking in a similar pace and tone and imagining stepping into the model of the world of the other person. Based on the findings of communication styles, the different styles favour different words. Therefore using similar key words and gestures without mimicking aligns better with their natural commu-nication style. To do this properly one needs to be subtle. It is not about being manipulative; rather it is about creating the best possible foundation for positive communication. The more unconscious rapport that is gained, the less likely a conversation can escalate into an argument.

Step 2

Mutually agree upon an outcome for the conversation. Make sure the outcomes are at a high level that results in either an understanding, gaining of clarity or an agreed position. An example of this would be an outcome where both parties reached a deeper understanding of one another, or that both parties felt heard and each had spoken their truth. Make a commitment to reaching this outcome instead of insist-ing upon being right. Keep in mind this self-coaching question: 'Would I rather be right or would I rather develop leadership communication skills that will serve me for a lifetime?' In any negotiation, the emotional response in either party is often triggered in a negative way. For those important negotiations, focus on the value, desires and perceptions of the other party; make sure both parties have already agreed on a target position, an acceptable position and a no-deal posi-tion. Once this is established, act less on emotive decisions and more on bringing value to all parties.

Step 3

Recognise that the only one that drives individual emotions is the individual themselves. Other people can influence emotions, but the captain of the personal mental and emotional ship is the individual. Often people trigger thoughts that are not about the actual situation, but linked to some key unresolved issues from the past. This is reflected when someone else's actions have an unusually strong and negative reactions in us over what would normally be considered reasonable. Each person needs to take reasonability for their own actions and reactions.

Help coach the other person from the use of victimised language by avoiding the use of language such as 'You make me . . .', 'You made me feel like . . .', 'You never . . .', 'You always . . .', 'Because you did that . . .', as these are outward-looking and blame-based statements. This is not taking responsibility for one's own responses, but trying to push it on to the other party, which will always have a negative reaction as the other party is placed into a defensive position. Most importantly, stop mindreading the other person's motives and limit personal assumptions. Take responsibility for the outcomes and keep focused on the results. Avoid language usage like 'I know what you were thinking . . .' or finishing their sentences for them.

Alternatively, utilise language such as 'I created for myself . . .', 'When you did that, I made up that you . . .'. Sometimes that relates to yourself and your feelings, like 'I choose to react like this . . .', or 'What I made up about you was . . .', 'How I interpreted that situation was . . .'

Hold both parties accountable to using upgraded language by taking full responsibility for how language and tone of voice is utilised. Remember to keep all sarcastic voice tonality out of the conversation. Avoid the pitfall of using damaging language or tones so that the energy is not wasted on defending oneself against linguistic attacks that distract from the heart and intention of the conversation. Be aware of tone of voice and energy behind the communication and manage the emotional responses. That is all one can control, and this will more rightly influence the other party.

Step 4
Remember to breathe. Breathing through the nose and exhaling through the mouth will lower the heart rate and bring more oxygen to the brain. This will enable a calmer and more focused state.

View each conversation as a golden opportunity to evolve self-leadership. Take the next opportunity with enthusiasm so the process becomes easier, forming a habit through repetition. When one analyses personal defensive positions, often there is a realisation that a victim mentality has been dominating the focus. Victim mentality comes from not taking responsibility. View all difficult conversations as opportunities to experience how far the role of victim has been conquered and moved into accountability. It is during the hardest situations in life that people learn the most; hence the most difficult conversations have the most learning potentials.

Clarify the other person's views with appreciative inquiry. Be as committed to understanding their perspective as possible and stand committed to reaching the agreed outcome for the conversation. Ask questions such as 'Can you clarify that last point?', or 'Can you speak a little more about that so I can understand your perspective a little better?'

Listen, reflect and take responsibility for creating the bridge to mutual understanding between any differences. Focus on gaining clarity. Avoid all sarcastic or demeaning tones in the voice and utilise only a sincere tone of voice within the questions and inquiries. Do not interrupt the other person when speaking and do not justify actions at any point in their turn to speak. Do not interrupt, just listen. Listen more than talk, and aim to hear the key messages.

Step 5

Be accountable and take ownership, particularly if difficulties arise, and don't place the blame on the other party or play victim. Identify personal contributions to the issue of the conversation and state your desire to resolve the issue. Look towards solutions and results, identifying what role you individually and collectively have, and agree on actions to be taken.

Ensure you avoid sympathy that is emotive and focus on understanding the other person's situation, but maintain the emotional strength to think logically towards the best possible solution. Empathy is one of the key by-products of the authentic conversation, because many individuals have never been truly heard and acknowledged without criticism.

Statements like 'I can understand how you can feel like you do and how you see the situation like you do', fundamentally acknowledge the person's model of the world and their perception is validated.

Step 6

At the end of the conversation, acknowledge what was learnt and acknowledge the other person for holding the conversation. Ensure it ends with an agreement, actions to progress as next steps, or make a time for the next conversation.

Legal-based agreements will be followed up with some legal instrument, whereas action lists lead to clarification to the next steps. Each action should have a responsible person as actions are designed to enable results with accountability. Create a commitment to hold each other accountable to any agreement.

The 12 Great Questions for Relationship Health

The art of the question is a powerful tool to utilise in keeping the conversation powerful, authentic and productive. Questions are often one of the best ways of gathering information and gaining clarity about a subject. Additionally, questions can invoke change in another person's perspective by opening new ways of considering alternative directions when thinking gets stuck. During a conversation there will be many opportunities to ask questions that will help gain greater clarity about an opposing position, so better understanding can be established.

Here are a variety of coaching questions to help the listener ask the right questions to achieve the conversational outcomes:

1. What do we require to speak about that would lead us to solution?

2. What do you require of me?

3. What has to happen to return us to clarity/understanding/ solution?

4. Do you desire to be right or to practise self-leadership?

5. What are the possibilities we can create together?

6. What are we really afraid of in our conversation?

7. What is your outcome from our conversation?

8. How many different ways can we look at this situation?

9. Most importantly, how does our position align with our individual values?

10. What are we not seeing here, what are our blind spots?

11. What possibilities can be created through better understanding?

12. Who do we both require to be, to create a solution that benefits everyone?

When the art of the authentic conversation is laced with well-thought-out questions and practiced, this skill becomes a great ally in invoking powerful, thoughtful conversations that evolve each person equally. Following a process can help prepare individuals for those long-awaited conversations that have acted like energy drains upon the mind and emotions.

Unfortunately in the workplace, when difficult conversations are seen as an avoidable consequence to life, a slow and steady decline in leadership growth and self-esteem becomes the end result. People simply ignore the situation, but it rarely goes away as it results in a breakdown in respect.

To help move past the blockages of fear created by past failed conversational attempts, recognise that action needs to be taken. Ignored issues grow, and the problem can get out of hand before management realises it. By following a fear-based strategy, people can further condition themselves into the pattern of avoidance rather than action and leadership. Knowing the consequences of withholding communication means leaders need to identify the conversations that must be held in order to develop personal leadership and take action.

The Jewel of Courage

When we invest in authentic conversations, authenticity blossoms and leaders receive the greatest possible return for the investment. The consequences include enriched character and stronger self-esteem and less stress. If conversations are ignored the situation remains unresolved in the mind and stress factors build.

Through deepened relationships, people strengthen positive relationships that can secure sustainable success therefore embracing one of the key principles of a humanistic business in the talent management cycle. When goals become achievable, opportunities increase and the ability to achieve results fast becomes supercharged, leading to a life of fulfilment. Just one tiny step towards authenticity can bring an individual immeasurable results for the better. Is it scary to hold conversations where vulnerability will be revealed? Admittedly, it's difficult to manage emotions and stop projection. However, the price that is paid for dysfunctional relationships based upon dysfunctional conversational strategies is much too high. Businesses can be destroyed by dysfunctional teams. This is perhaps the best investment a professional could ever make: the investment in leadership development and relationship skills.

Authentic conversations, both in professional and personal settings, are the doorways to how our evolution as an individual and leader deepens into character. Every conversation moves a person closer to success, but if façade-based conversations occur, then the result will be failure.

The authentic conversation establishes positive relationships that are key to success. The practice replicates positive communication experiences among members of a team or organisation and builds a strong culture where people thrive and feel emotionally safe. This positive culture reflects out into the market as a stronger endearing brand that attracts more business.

Establishing a healthy culture based upon longstanding, trusted relationships is the heart and soul of humanistic business, because people will do business with people who behave with integrity, especially those they like and trust. This all begins with the conversation.

Key Lessons

1. Success is determined by the success of our communication.
2. The quality of the conversation is in direct proportion to the success of relationships.
3. When the truth is withheld and communication deteriorates, the relationship slowly dies.
4. Every difficult conversation is a golden opportunity to build leadership and to personally evolve.

5. Establish a positive intention for all conversations and hold to that intention, making sure it is in alignment with professional and personal values.
6. Listen more, reflect on what's being said, do not interrupt and ask powerful questions to gain clarity.
7. Stay in physiological rapport during the conversation and remember to breathe.
8. Beliefs that support an authentic conversation include:
   - the map is not the territory;
   - relationships are mirrors where a person can see what cannot normally be seen about themselves;
   - relationships are meant to evoke the blind spots in our personality so evolution and growth can occur;
   - empathy is leadership power;
   - there is a positive intention behind behaviour;
   - there are no failures, only feedback;
   - flexibility in behaviour and perception is a fundamental key to success; and
   - respect each person's perspective and model of the world.

---

[1]. Mehrabian, A. (1971). *Silent Messages* (1st ed.).Belmont, CA: Wadsworth. ISBN 0-534-00910-7.

Chapter 8

People Intelligence

OVERVIEW

- People intelligence is critical to engaging and communicating with stake-holders.
- Building rapport with others is done through body language, the way we speak, our active listening skills and the language we use.
- Body language plays a critical role in personal likeability.
- Knowing human representational systems, such as seeing, hearing, feeling, etc., enables us to engage at the deepest possible level with people.

People intelligence impacts the space of talent management, values, purpose and methodology of the humanistic business model. Because so much of the foundation of a humanistic business is relational, our emphasis rests on understanding the diversity of people, utilising every tool available to discover the deep and enriched complexities of human nature so the very best can be invoked from every individual. When individuals perform, their energy has an influence on others and when the group has united aims, the group's performance increases as well. The only exception is when unhealthy competition is created within the team, where the vested interest of self-performance prevails over group outcomes.

The internal relationships of an organisation contribute to the creation of its culture, and are felt by external stakeholders through the attitude and brand energy in the marketplace at every touch point between the organisation and its customer. To build trusting relationships, both internal and external to the organisation, a new awareness and depth of understanding people is required. Relationship health rests with the foundation of great communication skills, authentic conversations and self-leadership practice.

Increasing people intelligence skills brings awareness to the subtle nuances of communication helping each leader master the authentic conversation strategy, improve staff relationships and enhance sales performance.

Very little of what comprises effective communication and influence is actually within the words that are used, but in the distinct, yet mysterious non-verbal cues of how people respond with their bodies, facial inflections, voice tone, tempo modulations and language. This is why when people are not being authentic, there are many signs that give them away.

Success in personal and professional relationships is based largely upon the ability to communicate effectively. Interestingly, the least trustworthy measure of the meaning of another's communication is in what they say, while the most trusted is what their body does and what is revealed through the subtle use of body language and its nuances. The ability to understand, read and respond to the subtle forms of communication from another person is the heartbeat of people intelligence and the foundation to make authentic conversations successful. When one can combine the messages in the words, tonality and body language and look for congruency, an individual can see the key messages and the underpinning motives and intent faster. People inherently have a sense of what body language means. However, research has shown that it's necessary to observe a combination, or cluster, of individual body postures before a conclusive judgment can be made. No single movement can be assumed to have a meaning, and three or more body language factors, with consideration to the context of the conversation, provide a solid basis to make conclusions that can then be tested for validity.

Staff within an organisation can be likened to the cells in the human body in that they must communicate effectively to perform different functions. When the body is healthy these cells are communicating and transferring information for the benefit of the organism to which they belong. When cells become unhealthy, they begin to miscommunicate or contaminate other associated cells and systems within their sphere of influence. Just like in the body, the disease of projection and misunderstanding can spread until the organisation, or organism, becomes ill. If these unhealthy cells go unaddressed and the disease is allowed to spread through neglect, then eventually the organisation fails, or the organism dies.

According to the Heart Math Research Institute,[1] each individual emanates a resonate field of energy beyond their own body that is now measurable by science. This field affects other people as far as 15 feet from them. This resonate field is controlled by the overall emotional state the person is feeling continually. From a humanistic business perspective, the culture can be likened to the collective emotional states of its internal stakeholders.

Their individual thoughts, as well as their language that represents those thoughts, the emotions they produce and the behaviours that ensue are all influencing factors on others. It only takes a few negative team members to influence the group, or impact the user experience of the customer.

The purpose of increasing people intelligence is to create more effective communication not only in the authentic conversational process but in the communication between staff members and customers. Positive people create positive energy and collectively can create an enormous brand energy and thriving culture. People intelligence creates the flexibility to honour the diversity of other people's perspectives so that personal differences are honoured with grace. The development of people intelligence is as vital to improved performance as self-leadership and emotional intelligence. People not only require the development of empathy and an understanding of self, but additionally need to know the subtle nuances of how to understand others so communication strategically moves towards mutual understanding.

There will always be difficult personalities and opposing behavioural styles to deal with and vital conversations to have. Often great results can be achieved, and when that is not possible, those relationships and conversations will point us in the direction of establishing boundaries and taking corrective actions. All relationships, both difficult and cooperative, are an opportunity to demonstrate self-leadership combined with people intelligence.

To increase people intelligence begin the exploration of the important distinctions about communication, non-verbal communications and creating understanding between the diversity of people's views and perspectives. The first step is to understand the key communication characteristics and the differences in styles of communication that people have.

In 1971, Albert Mehrabian's research concluded that there were three elements in any face-to-face communication:[2] words, tone of voice and body language. He found that our liking for a person who puts the message across is weighted in three categories:

  7 per cent for the words we use (verbal);
  38 per cent for the tone of voice we use (vocal); and
  55 per cent for the body language we convey (visual).

Body language appears to have the largest impact on how we begin to evaluate others. It's often said that people create a judgment on other people within a couple of minutes. So the first and arguably most important aspect of increasing our people intelligence is understanding body language remembering that our body language takes into consideration our dress as well.

Although the study of body language dates back thousands of years, there have been many new developments in recent years in understanding how emotional states affect our communication and physical health, and many books published on the subject. In *The Secret Language of Your Body,*[3] Inna Segal delves into the different aspects of the body and its meaning. In *Face Reading,*[4] Robert Whiteside writes extensively about reading the face. But it was Julius Fast, author of *Body Language,*[5] who was one of the very first individuals to bring the subject of body language to the forefront of the mainstream general public. And in more recent years, Australian body language expert Allan Pease drew attention to its significance in relationships.

Body language is part of the study of human evolution and is influenced both by inherited aspects and environmental influences which cause us to interpret non-verbal and verbal communication in the way that we do.

An important aspect of body language is facial expression and facial features, and 3,000 years ago, face reading was utilised as a system of diagnostics in Chinese medicine. The study of body gestures and movements, as well as eye patterns and voice tonality, is a more recent development, and the most in-depth studies of these aspects of body language have been carried out by the many contributors to the science of Neuro Linguistic Programming.

Knowing some commonly interpreted meanings of body gestures can help the understanding of some of the unconscious gestures and movements that people make, which reveal a deeper insight into their emotional world. Remember that no single gesture should constitute a meaning. At least three indicators, known as a cluster, need to exist before a judgment can be assumed. The cluster can include comparing the gesture to the context of the conversation. The individual movements that are recognised as part of a cluster include the following:

Nose touch – the gesture of deception. Can be done subtly by wiping, touching, scratching, or even pushing spectacles up or down on the nose.

Mouth guard – the gesture that signals we have said an untruth or we suspect some else is telling us an untruth. This is when a hand covers half of the mouth while talking.

Eye rub – a subconscious act that signals disapproval, or if done to avoid eye contact it is generally a sign of a feeling of inferiority.

Neck rub – a signal of increased stress, frustration, anger or a feeling of being overwhelmed.

Ear tug – a signal of impatience, disbelief or even displeasure, telling the speaker that the listener has heard enough.

Mouth cover – a gesture to show disagreement with the speaker, where a hand covers the whole of the mouth.

Steepling – a joined hand gesture, where both hands are held in a steepled position, signifies a feeling of superiority.

Shielding – a gesture that is used in an attempt to hide nervousness or shyness.

Ankle lock – a gesture to disguise nervousness.

Body cross – where the arms are crossed, signifying defensiveness or lack of a feeling of safety.

Hands on hips – a position of readiness, perhaps aggression.

Hand to cheek – thinking and/or evaluating.

Hand rubbing – anticipation.

Fondling of the hair – signifies a lack of self-confidence, insecurity.

Stroking the chin – attempting to make a decision.

One of the first steps, and one that is vital to authentic communication, is the ability to build trust by creating an unconscious physiological rapport with another person. Rapport is perhaps one of the most important ingredients to add to the mix of skills required in increasing our people intelligence. Rapport is a state of responsiveness that is created and established through matching another person's physiology, language and representational systems. The purpose of gaining rapport is to blur the boundaries around the differences between two people so a sense of emotional safety can be created, therefore allowing trust to be established.

As mentioned earlier, physiological rapport can be created by matching or mirroring the other person's body positioning and subtly reflecting back to them their own unconscious physical movements. Matching is when a person uses gestures and body positions utilising the same side of their body as the other person whereas mirroring is to form a mirror image of them by matching gestures and body positions utilising the opposite side of the body to them. Matching is used primarily in a more professional setting and mirroring in a more therapeutic setting. Here, the focus will be upon the process of matching.

For example, when one person desires to create unconscious rapport with another they can follow some simple steps to match the other person. If they are sitting with their legs crossed, then cross the lower part of your body too, not exactly in the same way, but similar. Have them sit first so you can enter into a similar position. If the other person is very expressive and makes lots of hand gestures when speaking, then when it's your turn to respond in the conversation, move your hands and gesture in a similar way, but understated rather than exact. If you are too obvious and exact in your matching, then you begin mimicking and that may be interpreted as offensive. Remember, being subtle is the key. Matching and mirroring can be full or partial, such as when two people have crossed arms for a full match, as opposed to one having crossed arms and the other crossed wrists to make a partial match.

To test the level of rapport, follow the movements of the other person until rapport is established, and then change your movement to test the rapport. This is called pacing and leading, and it happens when we lead by changing our body language and their physiology soon follows. If they follow your movement then you have established unconscious rapport. The importance of rapport is based on the theory that when people are 'like' each other, they 'like' each other and feel better understood and more comfortable.

The influence of effective communication and its place in creating trust and repeatable positive experiences for both internal and external stakeholders cannot be overemphasised. There's a far greater chance that communication will improve when people know and understand the strategies of how others communicate to build trust and rapport.

Some people are naturals at creating unconscious rapport, and it tends to be influenced by their natural behavioural and communication styles. Developing these skills will bring awareness to the processes and nuances of excellence in communication so that one can act in a consistent, repeatable and positive manner, and more strategically.

To deepen the understanding of how people communicate and add an extremely useful tool to increase people intelligence, the subject of human representational systems is the next step in this journey. This used to be referred to as our natural communication style, and it comes from the science of Neuro Linguistic Programming. The purpose of understanding another person's representational system is to be able to model precise communication into their preferred learning style so they feel heard, understood and listened to, thereby building additional trust and doing it faster and more effectively.

There are three primary human representational systems and two secondary ones, which make up the five senses. The primary systems are visual (our seeing ability), auditory (hearing ability) and kinaesthetic (feeling ability), which are represented both in physical sensations and emotional feelings. Often the auditory system can be divided into auditory or auditory digital. Auditory digital is not a direct sensory input system; rather it acts as a filter for people to make sense out of what has come through the five senses. It's often witnessed by observing how a person may begin talking to themselves as they think through the task at hand. The secondary systems are olfactory sense, or sense of smell, and the gustatory system, which is the sense of taste.

We'll be addressing how these five senses and preferred representational systems affect communication. People utilise all these five sensory systems daily in how they experience their world. However, people have their own preferred representational styles that govern communication and their internal processing. To understand the distinctions of how an individual prefers to represent their internal world, tells volumes about their nature, temperament and communication preferences.

The first primary representational system, visual processing, can represent an enormous amount of data simultaneously and instantaneously. That's why the visual system is helpful, because it enables massive amounts of data to be processed rapidly. Here are some of the distinctions of a person who prefers the visual system. Generally they:

1. stand or sit erect or lean forwards with their eyes up;

2. breathe at the top of their lungs;

3. are organised, neat, well groomed and orderly;

4. memorise by seeing pictures and are less distracted by noise;

5. have difficulty remembering verbal instructions and their mind often wanders; and

6. focus on their appearance – how things look is important to them.

The second primary representational system is the auditory system. Auditory processing is sequential and takes longer than visual processing. Here are some of the distinctions of a person who prefers the auditory system. Generally they:

1. tend to move their eyes laterally;

2. breathe in their mid-chest;

3. enjoy verbal praise, music and talking on the phone;

4. learn by hearing verbal instructions and are distracted by noise;

5. exhibit a tendency to talk to themselves and even move their lips; and

6. are more interested in what you say and how you say it, being sensitive to the tone and timber of your voice.

The third primary representational system is the kinaesthetic system. This is a feelings-based person. Kinaesthetic touch provides the raw data, such as tactile qualities and temperature. Kinaesthetic feelings are the overriding emotional responses that are the primary way people evaluate their experiences, and they usually have a positive or negative value. It's often referred to as someone's intuition. These emotions, or feeling states, can be created through association from past experiences or belief systems.

Here are some of the distinctions of a person who prefers the kinaesthetic system. Generally they:

1. have their eyes looking down, tapping into their feelings;

2. tend to walk slower;

3. breathe from the lower lungs, often resulting in their clothes moving around their stomach;

4. pick up on the emotive aspects in language;

5. connect to people through touch; and

6. prefer comfortable clothing.

When attempting to determine another person's representational preference, there are several methods that can be utilised to match human representational styles with how they prefer to receive communication. In addition to matching physiology and being aware of what the body is doing to determine someone's representational preferences, language usage also gives valuable insights into a person's communication preferences.

Visual people will often use language that favours visual attributes, such as, 'I see what you're saying', 'I can picture that', 'The future looks bright' or 'It was glaringly obvious'. Auditory people will favour sound attributes, and may say, 'It sounds right to me', 'It doesn't ring true', 'Does this resonate with you?' or 'It's as clear as a bell'. Kinaesthetic people favour feelings-based attributes, and may use phrases like, 'It boils down to one thing', 'I get the drift of', 'Let's get in touch with', 'Let's grab hold of the problem', 'Pain in the neck' or 'Sharp as a tack'.

When responding to a visual, auditory or kinaesthetic person in a conversation, ideally you want to match their linguistic and representational distinctions, as well as their key words and phrases. The more you are able to match their physiology and language, the more seamless your rapport-building skills will become.

It was John Grinder and Richard Bandler, the co-founders of Neuro Linguistic Programming, who first identified a relationship between sensory-based language and eye-accessing cues. These cues are idiosyncratic and habitual for each person and offer indications as to how the person is processing or representing a problem unconsciously. It can reflect whether they are thinking in pictures, sounds or feelings, as well as if they are engaging in internal dialogue (talking to themselves). Eye movements will reveal whether a person sorts visually, auditorially or kinaesthetically. When the eyes move up, the individual is sorting visually; when they look laterally, they are sorting auditorially; and when they look down, they are sorting kinaesthetically.

While some left-handed individuals have a reverse mapping a person can have the left and right indicators on the opposite side to the diagram shown. Most people's map is the same, so you need to test this by asking questions you know the answers to to confirm the responses as a form of calibration, before you rely on the indications. The following diagram represents the mapping from the viewer's perspective.

Vc Visual Construct /Create
Vr Visual Recall / Remembered
Act Auditory Construct / Create/ Tonal
Art Auditory Recall / Remembered/ Tonal
K Kinaesthetic (Feelings)
Aid Processing (Auditory Digital / Internal Dialogue)

By watching the other person's eye movements (specifically the fast movement of the pupil and not necessarily where they end up staring), one can determine which quadrant of the eye pattern chart their eyes move to, which represents the part of the brain they are utilising. The most dominantly used area can give an indication of their visual, auditory or kinaesthetic preferences.

In addition, the tempo and cadence of their language are important distinctions of the three primary representational systems, so be mindful that visual people will generally speak faster and process information more quickly. To create rapport one would need to match the pace at which the conversation is moving. Auditory people will prefer a musical rhythm-type quality to the voice with a tempo that is less quick, but moving to the same rhythm.

Kinaesthetic people will prefer a slower pace to the tempo of the conversation and will lose interest in the conversation if the conversation moves too fast with lots of information. With kinaesthetic people, one would need to reduce rapid-fire conversations with lots of detail to a slower tempo and allow a kinaesthetic person to absorb the information from the conversation before carrying on with more information. They will want time to process the content of the discussion, to check in with their feelings.

Once rapport has been established, and representational systems identified and matched, the primary focus needs to be on the conversation itself and the language being used. This introduction to the awareness of linguistic usage is a vast study of the power of language and the words people use. Linguistics and the assumptions that lie underneath a person's word choices are critically important. Language symbolises experiences and represents them in our thinking, which influences our speech expression. The quickest way to gain clarity about another person is to listen to the word choices they use in a conversation. Listening for this deeper structure of language is a vital skill in increasing people intelligence and therefore communication mastery. The purpose of listening for the deep structure is to understand what can be logically assumed by the word choices the speaker has utilised. This type of listening allows a peek into the inner world of the speaker's thinking strategies and brings understanding to their emotional propensities.

The ability to listen at this level gives us the edge in directing a meaningful conversation so we can quickly discover the heart of the matter. In fact, linguistic models such as the meta-model have determined finite patterns in the use of language, and highlights where information may be missing, or the typical responses required to rapidly identify the person's deep challenges. This will be a brief introduction to these patterns as it is an extensive study in language patterns. These identified language patterns were based on the work of the mother of family therapy Virginia Satir. The meta-model follows the idea that language is a translation of mental states into words, and that not everything may be said (deletion), there may be underlying assumptions and structural inadequacies (distortions) and it may reflect a shift towards more universal and absolute statements (generalisations). These psycho-linguistic adaptations are what make the science of artificial intelligence so complex in trying to get computers or robots to mimic human communications, as computers need to have a base of absolute references to work from, and not ambiguous embedded messages. There are 10 key categories that have been identified.

Category	Comparator
Comparative Deletion	Comparator
Unspecified Referential Index	Referential Index Specified
Unspecified Verb	Specified Verb
Nominalisations	Specified Verb
Simple Deletion	Deletion Response
Universal Qualifier	Counter Example
Modal Operator	Complex Equivalent
Cause and Effect	Subjectively Identified Cause
Mind Read	Projected Effect
Lost Performer	Performer

The meta-model requires extensive study, but it shows how an experienced coach, trouble-shooter or trained negotiator can get to the core issues or beliefs fast. Take the example of a person saying 'This always happens to me'. This statement would be categorised as a universal qualifier, and the trained coach would simply need to respond with a counter example, such as 'Have you ever experienced a day where this did not happen to you?' to begin to challenge the universality of the statement and bring to light that the events do not 'always happen' honouring that it may be experienced as a constant however it is indeed not a constant. It shifts the conversation to the core issue which is the globalisation and generalisation of the statement.

Here is another example of a cause and effect statement and its linguistic challenge: 'Because he said that to me I got really defensive.' The trained coach could reply: 'How did what he said cause you to choose to become defensive?' This question returns the responsibility of the emotional response back to the speaker and returns them to being at cause rather than victim.

Each category from the Meta Model represents ways that individuals think and use language with a specific way of responding to reveal the missing information and challenge the thinking position. In a humanistic business there is a focus on talent management and up-skilling management to bring the best forth from the people they lead. This one skill is an important skill for coaching others or creating conversations that can change attitudes. Managers perfecting these models can quickly and effectively dive to the core issues in record time.

People's language is the doorway into their emotional world. There exists a set of simple yet important questions that an individual can use to help create better understanding by thinking about language differently. Language usage is a powerful influencer on the emotional world of an individual.

Most organisations choose to motivate staff, hoping to turn them into enthused advocates of their brand. By understanding the power of language and the deeper meaning of what language choices reveal, a manager can help improve an individual's performance through having the capacity to address the core issues, rather than over-empathising or not really listening to what is beneath the words, and never addressing the root cause of the issues.

When ineffective conversations occur, trust can be broken and the manager loses credibility and effectiveness with staff. To evolve this people intelligence, a leader needs to develop their rapport skills through physiological matching and representational system usage, as well as through linguistic usage and what that usage presupposes.

To begin developing this skill, ask the following questions of yourself:

- What has to be true at an emotional level for them to have said that?
- What emotions would drive those word choices?
- What can be assumed to be the emotional driver underneath the obvious emotions?

For example, if anger is present, ask yourself, 'What is the emotion underneath the anger that drives the anger?' If the surface emotion is anger, often the emotion underneath anger is hurt. Underneath hurt is often rejection, a feeling of betrayal for not being valued or loved. It is never about the anger itself, but the driving emotions underneath the anger that is the important element to address.

When a manager or leader understands this, they can help the individual identify options and lead the person to create alternatives in perception and behaviour. This knowledge is a necessary requirement to developing people intelligence, understanding, empathy, compassion and best-practice communication. When a leader listens for the emotional presuppositions inherent in another person's language, they awaken to a new way of perceiving and discovering ways to motivate team members. The ability to have insight, empathy and compassion for another's situation will rapidly increase, as will the effectiveness of the communication. Individuals will also find they become less judgmental, creating more emotional safety and more willingness to hold deep authentic conversations.

Non-leadership behaviours and communication are generally motivated by fear in its myriad forms. A lack of emotional and mental management will lose the respect and trust of teams, associates and customers. People do business with people they know, like and trust and whom they perceive to act with integrity.

When one responds with understanding for another at the level of their deeper emotional driver, they can go straight to the heart of the matter rather than holding conversations about their behaviour. When a conversation is held about the emotion that is driving the behaviour, the true cause can come to light and resolution can be addressed. This is where real change and assistance can take place. Why would anyone expect to create resolution by addressing the symptom without dealing with the cause?

Increase people intelligence and hold conversations from a position of care, understanding and curiosity, rather than criticism, prosecution and blame. When this shift occurs, trust evolves, repeatable positive experiences happen and enthused advocates are born in the ranks of the organisation.

People are not intrinsically slackers, blockers or fundamentally bad, but are often simply responding to their motivation to avoid pain or dealing with their fears. When people are afraid, they often behave in ways that are not favourable. It is always a choice to enter conversations with people intelligence, reflecting a deeper set of values and a greater will to engage, connect and support one another with insight and tools for motivating. This approach will build leadership, brand power and organisational health and wellbeing, whereas its alternative will cut at the root of an organisation's best efforts to obtain and maintain success.

Key Lessons

1. People intelligence is a pillar for effective communication.
2. Each person is responsible for their thinking and therefore their emotional states. Each person contributes to the overall wellbeing of the culture they belong to.
3. One person can contaminate an entire productive team.
4. 7 per cent of our communication is represented by words;
5. 38 per cent by the tone of our voice; and
6. 55 per cent by the physiology we utilise during our conversations.
7. Rapport is essential for establishing trust.
8. The three primary representational systems are visual, auditory and kinaesthetic.
9. Language and eye patterns are key indicators of the representational systems and thinking patterns of the speaker.
10. Practice listening for the deep structure inherent in a person's language usage.

1. McVarthy R. Phd, Heart Math Research Center, Institute of Heart Math, Publication No.02-035 Boulder Creek, CA. 2002

2. Mehrabian, A. (1971). *Silent Messages* (1st ed.).Belmont, CA: Wadsworth. ISBN 0-534-00910-7.

3. Segal, I. (2010). *The Secret Language of Your Body: The Essential Guide to Health and Wellness*, Atria Books.

4. Whiteside, R. (1992). *Face Language: A Guide to Meeting the Right Person*, Frederick Fell Publishing.

5. Fast, J. (2002). *Body Language*, M. Evans and Company.

Chapter 9

Aligning Products and Services

OVERVIEW

- Products comprise the physical products, services and offerings that generate revenue to sustain the business.
- Products need to be designed in alignment with the values and ethos of the business, including how they are delivered.
- The team involved in the end-to-end production to delivery processes includes suppliers and their selection is also critical to the business delivering on its promises.
- The point where the customer interfaces with team members, often referred to as customer service, is a critical engagement step in building long-term relationships.
- Products that are designed well and positioned to do good in the world often enable a commitment by the customer to pay more.

Businesses exist by attracting income through their products and services. Without income, the business cannot survive, and so the ability to attract prospects, then convert them to customers and retain them is the ultimate aim of an organisation. Humanistic business is committed to generating sustainable growth, contribution and financial profit through aligning all external and internal stakeholders under the umbrella of a common vision and mission. Every aspect of the business must demonstrate its corporate soul, resulting in an appropriate range of goods or service that effectively meets the needs and demands of its clientele.

Products and services are the offerings that a business makes to its customers and, for the purposes of this chapter, the term 'products' is used to encompass all revenue-generating physical products and human-resource-based services.

Product delivery is where the collective effectiveness of the business's values, systems and processes, team and branding all come together at the intersecting point where the business delivers to its paying customers. This means that the products need to be developed in alignment with the purpose and ethos of the business.

The reputation of a business is directly linked to the quality of its products, and the real or perceived value that they bring. Humanistic businesses know that their products reflect their image and enhance their stakeholder relationships. They understand that good experiences with these products lead to customer satisfaction, repeat business and referrals.

Having a higher purpose and doing good creates great business success and lasting sustainability and generates more opportunity to grow and give something back into the communities the organisation serves. While humanistic businesses are very values-focused in offering information, gifts and services that do not result in immediate payment, they have other benefits that increase brand awareness, and create interest, trust and respect with other stakeholders. Humanistic businesses recognise that planting these seeds leads to revenue-generating business in the future. As an example, Cisco Systems, which is a multi-international organisation, takes its corporate responsibility seriously by focusing on issues such as education, combating poverty and improving health care in the countries in which it operates. John Chambers, CEO of Cisco Systems, was awarded the prestigious Inaugural Clinton Global Citizen Award for spearheading a number of programs that were primarily focused on using technology to increase global education and socio-economic development, as well as addressing the fundamental needs surrounding poverty, such as providing food, water and shelter in poverty-stricken areas around the globe. The results of doing good and having a product and service that also reflects the commitment to social responsibility is echoed in John Chambers' comments about Cisco's philanthropic efforts in the Middle East: 'Companies should only do what is in the best interest of their shareholders, employees, customers and society as a whole. It's a balancing act. And so I am a believer that you should do what's right, because it is the right thing to do. But it's also good for business. And it's important for business to understand that.'[1]

If a good percentage of growth in emerging markets happens through doing good, then why wouldn't every organisation do the right thing by the staff and the communities it serves? It all begins with one defining step that brings us back to tapping into our personal values. Values must be defined and reflected throughout the operations of the organisation. The mission statement that drives the vision can only be defined once the values have been defined. As in most accepted business practices, all too often, values are defined by top-level management from the industry's best-practice values. The danger in identifying values by industry standards is they can lack emotional engagement. If upper management members have yet to define their personal values, they may discover that these do not align with the industry-standard values.

The reality is that those stated values, if they were truly accepted values, should be looked upon as key principles that must be applied when making decisions. When an organisation creates a values list for the business, make sure there is personal buy-in and that decisions are made in compliance with them. This includes decisions on selecting products to go to market. Consistent adherence to value-driven systems and policies builds trust, culture and brand energy, which appeals to both internal and external stakeholders alike.

The products discussed in this section are more focused on the revenue-generating efforts of a business, noting that marketing-based products, or those given away, form part of the marketing strategy rather than product development for immediate income. In considering new products, a business must satisfy itself that there is a target market (target customer), that the target customer has a real need (customer need), that the proposed product will meet that need (fit for purpose), and the organisation has the means to design, produce and distribute that product in a cost-effective manner (ability to deliver). When any one of these conditions is not met, the commercial viability of the product must be questioned and compared to other alternative product options.

Design to a Market Need

The first critical step for a business is to confirm the market viability of the products it proposes to offer to a specified target market. In order to establish this, a 'markets needs analysis' should be prepared to ensure there is a market demand and a missing niche in the marketplace that requires filling, before proceeding to product development. The aim is not to create products that are personally desirable, but to create products that the market desires. Here are some fundamental questions to explore when defining product and service viability in the market:

- Is a target market clearly identifiable?

- What is the size of your target market and where is it located?

- What is the social, economic and demographic position of your target market and will potential customers recognise the need enough to engage?

- Has there been an assessment of the potential customers' needs?

- Can the unique quality of the product or service be duplicated that is being offered to the potential customer?

- How wide and deep an impact will this product have on their lives?

- What will attract potential customers to this product?

- Does the product or service reflect organisational values?

- What outrageous organisational guarantees can be offered about its quality?

- How long a market lead will there be before competitors start offering something similar?

- What is the brand difference between what is being offered and the competition?

- What are the pricing factors and the range of pricing?

- Can the price and the product's uniqueness create sustainability in an ever-changing marketplace?

- Are there any barriers to buying?

- What are the distribution channels and what are the potential barriers from production to market?

- What are the benefits that the product or service offers that the competition does not?

Answering these questions will result in a streamlined conceptual market needs assessment that will provide the evidence of the commercial feasibility of a product. Some additional benefits can result in a simplified explanation of how the product or service will be marketed, an estimated general price for the product and the projected response from the market.

When a product is in the process of discovery, it's important to verify that it adheres to the overall intent of the established values of the organisation and provides true value to the customer. When defining organisational values, not only is there an obligation to drive systems and policies forward through congruent adherence to what is believed, but additionally to align the right external stakeholders such as suppliers and distribution chains, to verify that the organisation is supporting and remaining congruent to its brand and its promise to its customers.

This includes examining the 'fit for purpose' element, which looks at the product's functionality, application, reliability and all aspects of quality. This must extend to its cosmetic look, ease of use, colour range and potential accessories. The business must look at the whole production and distribution process and in particular take responsibility for its marketing and ultimate delivery to the client.

A great example of this principle is Patagonia, an outdoor clothing company. Their brand is exemplified by their belief in their supply chain transparency, which they refer to as the Footprint Chronicles. They say: 'The Footprint Chronicles® examines Patagonia's life and habits as a company. The goal is to use transparency about our supply chain to help us reduce our adverse social and environmental impacts on an industrial scale. We've been in business long enough to know that when we can reduce or eliminate a harm, other businesses will be eager to follow suit.'[2]

This transparency instils deep trust in their customer base that their purchase causes the least amount of harm to people, animals and the environment and perhaps even suggests that purchasing Patagonian products may actually help the world rather than harm it any further. This results in greater production, loyal staff, a larger customer base and more profitable results than their competitors.

According to the research conducted by Rajendra Sisodia, Jag Sheth and David Wolfe in their book *Firms of Endearment*, Patagonia outperforms their competition by a margin of 50 per cent greater profit and their customers pay on average 20 per cent or more than their competitors' price.[3] Patagonia has successfully established themselves from the inside out, top to bottom, as a humanistic business throughout their branding. The consumer has matured, not only in how they create their choices, but in their inherent understanding that unless humanity begins the process of becoming aware of the impact that our collective choices have on each other and the environment, our future will be bleak.

Consider the following example where a health care company's brand was built on the mission and vision of supplying the most nutrient-rich food sources to their customers, but where they were found to be selling products from suppliers that used low standards in the production process or were heavily dependent on hazardous chemicals and pesticides to grow their products. Would they be congruent in their customer's eyes? In this case, there would be serious doubt that the end user's trust would grow for the health care company. The quality of the end product is jeopardised by the real or perceived quality of its production process.

If a supplier was inconsistent in their deliverables, which caused an interruption in the supply chain that resulted in an organisation's product being delayed, the brand would suffer, their reputation would falter and the trust of the customer impacted. All the effort up to the delivery point may have been exceptional, but the distribution process loses or frustrates the customer. This is why humanistic businesses consider the whole process, independent of whether they or a contractor delivers on a part of it.

It is not only a well-intended, values-driven CEO that creates a great company, but a combination of the values, systems and the finer distinctions of managing all the operations that creates the consistency for all those involved. This is one of the reasons the Apple company has its own shops and manages the whole user experience. The consistency consequently builds the trust of the customer that they will receive the same service and quality product every time they engage in doing business with the organisation.

Developing New Products

Apart from market need, products are developed through the innovative techniques already discussed that look towards solving problems, making processes faster, adding features, increasing functions, offering wider ranges (colours, sizes, etc.) or offering a completely new combination of existing elements.

Often innovation is found in analysing one industry and seeing how its strengths are applicable in another industry. Take the example of a car manufacture's distribution channels compared to those of a mining operation. They both need to take raw materials and transport them to a processing plant and then distribute the processed material to diverse parts of the world. The mining sector could likely learn from the car-manufacturing sector and vice versa. Sometimes it is not the actual things you witness that makes a difference, it is the thinking that is triggered that causes new thoughts.

We often become innovative by studying other industries and sectors, including the competition. In fact, smart business is not in reinventing the wheel, it's about taking others' ideas and building upon them, sometimes creating a best of breed solution. This is the concept of modelling, where an innovator looks at what the market leader is doing and mimics it to get similar results. What we are purporting is to investigate, analyse, take the good components, disregard or overcome the negative components, learn from others' experiences and mistakes and build upon all that knowledge to create a better, more efficient and effective organisation. Humanistic businesses excel in capturing customer feedback and ideas, and products or improvements can come from ideas from those with a need. Make sure to engage with the users and potential customers to find out their key hurts, needs, wants and desires and create products that fulfil those.

Extending the Team

One key factor in guaranteeing success and congruency in the trust-building process of the organisational brand is choosing the right suppliers to work with. This increases the confidence that the organisational values can be demonstrated from the start to the end of the process, and that a consistent quality can be delivered to the end user without interruption. To help identify appropriate suppliers, consider the following:

- **Reputation** – investigate the supplier's reputation in the marketplace. First, look at how competent the supplier actually is. Review the supplier's capabilities to meet your requirements. Make an assessment of whether they can deliver on time and with the consistency and quality you expect and require. Ask for references and speak to other customers to verify your evaluation is accurate and they do what they say they capable of doing. Check that the supplier's values are positioned to complement your operating values and review their website for their mission and values statement.

- **Capability** – check that the supplier has the resources to meet your requirements in the time constraints that your organisation operates within. Confirm that their supply chain remains adequately resourced to be able to adjust to your market variations on demand. Verify if they have enough qualified staff, delivery operations and systems as well as financial resources and materials to address an influx of business so your deliverable is still able to be on time, every time.

- **Service Consistency** – check that the supplier holds a history of customer service excellence in their field. Look for excellence in their list of values and an ever-present desire to improve their staff training and system modification to meet the needs of the changing market. Do they know how to run a project and are they trained in best-practice project management to enable a consistent and ever-improving implementation approach? The supplier also needs to have a high standard of customer service and a demonstrable willingness to provide excellent service over long-term projects as you continue to work together.

- **Financial Sustainability** – verify that the supplier has the financial health and wellbeing to navigate the financial ups and downs of conducting business in a stormy economy. This is especially important when entering into a long-term agreement with crucial suppliers.

Check that the deliverable can be supplied to the customer on time, no matter what. Verify that within the supply chain all suppliers and key players have the resources to meet the organisation's needs so the integrity of the promise to the customer stays consistent and can be delivered.

- **Reliability** – confirm that the supplier has the systems and procedures in place to provide a consistent and reliable delivery of their product or service. Ask the supplier to demonstrate their systems and procedures so they can be verified first-hand.

- **Positive Relationships** – check the supplier's past record in dealing with other businesses. The relationship factor is key in an on-going supplier relationship, so discuss how the communication will occur and how often, who is your key contact in the business relationship, how do they handle conflict resolution and mediation and when and in what form will the communication occur if a crisis occurs within the supply chain. Manage expectations up front and ask the hard questions early.

Once the values, mission and vision have been designed to embrace a humanistic philosophy and the product or service feasibility has been established, the research into the supplier chain can begin and, once completed, the true test in brand congruency begins.

Brand Congruency

At the heart of a humanistic business is brand congruency which is committed to an uncompromising consistency throughout all interactions and touch points between organisational marketing, staff and customer. In a humanistic business every touch point must exhibit its values and mission from the first point of contact, throughout the process of delivery, to completion of the product and on to the follow-up, feedback and the end-to-end user experience of the brand.

The ultimate example of branding expertise in a company, where no stone is left unturned in fulfilling the marketing and brand congruence, has to be Disney. If the layers of the marketing and brand genius that compiles the Disney marketing machine were to be unveiled there would lie at its foundation one powerful mission:

> 'The mission of The Walt Disney Company is to be one of the world's leading producers and providers of entertainment and information. Using our portfolio of brands to differentiate our content, services and consumer products, we seek to develop the most creative, innovative and profitable entertainment experiences and related products in the world.
>
> We believe we can achieve this goal by conducting our business and creating our products in an ethical manner, and by promoting the happiness and wellbeing of kids and families by inspiring them to join us in creating a brighter tomorrow.'[4]

Ultimately, the fulfilment of individual values results in happiness. At the heart of Disney's values and mission is the fulfilment of happiness in as many people on the planet as possible. Just think about the experience of going to one of the Disney World theme parks around the world. Firstly, the experience of expectation begins well before you even arrive at the theme park. Billboards announce the approach of your fantasy world miles ahead of the destination point where you are promised a place of fantasy, adventure and escape from the worries of your world.

The beginning vision of Walt Disney was 'to make people happy', and to his credit he has inspired an organisation that continues to place this core value at the forefront of their branding efforts and their product and services, way beyond his own life.

Whether you are a solo entrepreneur, a mid-sized business or an international global organisation, there is something to be learnt from Disney's attention to brand congruency, excellence in their products, delivery of their services and their deep desire to consistently deliver the message of happiness that is demonstrated even in the finest details of their operations.

Most organisations know that brand congruency infused into their products is vital to their sustainable success but often have not fully considered the different aspects of what constitutes their brand congruency. Here are some concepts to consider:

- Are the values and mission fully recognised by staff? Are these posted throughout the office and workplace?

- Is the website congruent with the organisational values and does it exhibit absolute transparency in how the values are demonstrated within the operations and supplier chain?

- Are the organisational values and mission vital aspects of the culture and is it necessary for all employees to adhere to those values in the workplace? Are they discussed in detail during the new recruitment induction process?

- Is the website created to be easy to navigate and understand, creating a friendly user experience that demonstrates the organisation's message and brand?

- Is the look of the advertising focused directly at the organisation's target market and does it have the emotional leverage to convince the customer to engage in the company's services?

- Is the advertising in alignment with the look and feel of the brand and does it capture the heart and soul of the organisational values visually and within its message?

- Are the staff empowered in their attitude to consistently be an advocate for the brand? Have they received enough training to be educated in self-leadership so they have the life skills to align their personal values with those of the organisation?

- Is every aspect of the appearance of the organisation well managed, from the appearance and decor of the offices to the cleanliness? Are the grounds well maintained and are the bathrooms clean? Do your staff appear professional and are they happy?

- Does the organisation conduct end-user experience surveys and other forms of feedback to discover any brand inconsistency in the sales and delivery chain, and are there any staff anomalies that require further training and correction? Is the organisation on the path of constant improvement?

- How does the organisation handle disputes and is the strategy in alignment with the overall values and mission of the organisation?

- Are the policies clearly defined for public access so the organisational policies and procedures are unquestionable? Are these discussed at the point of the sale so that each customer understands the choice they are making and clarity is established before the purchase?

- The best customers of an organisation are its guarantee of sustainability. How is the loyal customer rewarded? What incentives are given and how often? How does the organisation fulfil its best-practice customer-service protocols, from the first point of contact to securing an on-going relationship with each and every customer at every additional point of contact?

- One key element in the congruency of the brand delivery and loyalty to the product and service is customer service. It can cost an organisation four to six times as much in operational and training costs to win a new customer than it does to retain one.[5] So, the financial impact of good customer service can become the backbone of an organisation's sustainable future.

Service Excellence

Service excellence cannot be contained to just one department, but must be a pervasive attitude from the CEO to the front-desk phone operator. Great customer service reflects the values and mission of the organisation at every step and is more than a slogan on the staff canteen wall. Great customer service drives all systems and operational procedures and is deeply embedded in the hiring process so the human resource department selects the best candidates whose personal values align with the organisational values.

The following is a shortlist of some of the most important tips for great customer service:

1. Service should be the underpinning primary focus at all levels of the organisation.

2. Practice the art of kaizen, which is the constant focus on

continuous improvement, by using an end-user experience survey or other evaluation mechanism to obtain valuable feedback on any corrections required to the systems or improvements in staff training.

3. Invest in the human equity of the organisation to keep growing the soft skills of employees so their personal lives improve and their work performance expands, as the two go hand in hand.

4. Differentiate yourself from the competition through market analysis and product research.

5. Deliver the product and service through consistent, unique branding and rich user experiences so that every touch point from start to finish reflects the commitment to excellent service.

6. Use complaints as a vehicle for improving your products. Commit to honouring the feedback as a way of discovering any holes in the products, and let the complaining customer know how much the organisation values their input and business.

7. Ensure the management is capable of tackling problems that are identified and providing innovative solutions and ideas for improving the systems and operations.

8. Create a clear distinction between your brand and those of the competition so the consumer knows why they are buying from you and what the difference is.

9. Create powerful alliances with suppliers and treat them as one of the most valuable stakeholders in the organisation. They become family in the overall expression of how the organisation conducts business.

10. Use incentives to increase staff participation and attitudes so that high-performing team members are rewarded.

11. Leadership skills need to be taught at every level of the organisation, because sustainable leadership can only be built on the foundation of personal self-leadership.

12. Measure the results and the satisfaction of staff and customers.

13. Keep your word and always deliver on your promises.

14. Stick to the organisational values and avoid scarcity thinking.

15. Ban the use of negative language throughout all levels of the organisation and adopt the attitude of the language of possibility.

16. Know the customers and keep up with forecasted trends so the products remain ahead of the competition and match the changing market needs.

17. Make sure the organisation's guidelines are well defined for the customer service department staff so they are empowered to make decisions.

Additionally, train your customer service staff in the fine art of listening and asking the right questions. The objective is to create a sense of confidence in the customer that the organisation has respectfully listened, understood the problem or issue and has asked the right questions to get the desired results. It may be that the required resolution is not within the customer service representative's scope of authority, so they need to know when to refer to a higher level and to remain in the loop until the customer is connected and properly handed over to the specialist.

When the values of the organisation include service excellence, it's vital to teach the customer service team how to demonstrate patience as a necessary skill. When a customer is speaking, the representative must allow them to finish explaining their issue before they attempt to create a resolution. They should always show respect by listening fully and to check that they have understood the customer before any attempt is made to resolve the issue.

In a humanistic business, training in self-leadership is essential for all departments, but more so for the customer service team. It's imperative that all customer service representatives know the emotional and mental management techniques of self-leadership so they can separate one customer call from another. If they receive an angry or abusive call they need the ability to separate the impact of that call from the next call and manage their emotional state to avoid the transference of emotions from one customer to the next.

An organisation's profit centre is not necessarily in the top-level board-room, but at the front line where team members engage directly with the consumer. Consequently, the customer service department can become the organisation's gold mine or its Achilles heel.

It takes a strong management commitment to excellence, tenacity and a never-ending drive for success that when infused with human-ity and a concern for the wellbeing of all, creates an unstoppable power for good. As John Chambers from Cisco so aptly put it: 'The key message here is that doing good is not only right, it's the right thing for business.'

Pricing Strategy

Most business operators undervalue their products and position them-selves low in the price range and therefore in the most competitive space. Evidently, the small corner shop cannot compete with the big players on price.

According to the research of neurologist Antonio Damasio from the USC College of Brain and Creativity Research Centre, people do not make their decisions on reason or even price, but on how they feel.[6] Customers are loyal to a brand when they feel an emotional connec-tion, and trust is built through consistent positive experiences at every touch point of their experience during the sales process.

Those businesses perceived to be doing good in the world can charge higher prices, as consumers feel good in supporting good behaviour. Remember the example of the 20 per cent higher cost of buying free-range eggs over factory-farmed ones. The customer feels more comfortable that the chickens are being treated more humanely and are prepared to pay the higher price for that emotional state. Of course, the costs to the business go up, but so does the price paid by the customer, meaning that the price of doing good can often be passed to the end consumer, as a kind of teamwork in doing good.

Successful businesses are no longer reliant on price wars to create their brand distinction, because that approach only attracts customers looking for the best price, not long-term loyalty. When a product is infused with a humanistic brand, the customer believes in it and has established an emotional connection with it, and that organisation has likely created a customer for life.

This success methodology establishes consistent loyalty to a product that endears itself to the consumer by creating an offering out of a heartfelt concern to do good, by all stakeholders, both internal and external.

An Enduring Culture for Product Improvement

All changes in an organisation have a direct impact on its products and delivery mechanisms. From the top-down approaches of management to the bottom-up ideas of its team members, success needs to incorporate the whole team working in unison.

When product development takes into account the needs of the end customer, coupled with consideration for the whole design and manufacture process and its wider impact on people, animals and society, then the focus is truly humanistic.

Carry out internal reviews, get external feedback and speak with customers on a regular basis. Pay attention to the consistency of people empowerment, cultural improvement and end-user satisfaction and offer guarantees that support quality and build trust with your customers. Tangible products often outlive the life of a business, so make everyone count in protecting a reputation to be proud of.

The search for excellence in organisational change is a never-ending process involving careful judgment of the effect on all internal and external stakeholders. If an organisation is seeking long-term loyal customers who are advocates for the brand and make repeat purchases, then creating congruent, dependable, values-driven products is the only sustainable strategy for success in the newly emerging humanistic capitalism of tomorrow.

Key Lessons

1. Customer service team members must be trained in self-leadership to enable effective engagement with customers each time.
2. Product development must be based on having an identified target customer and a recognised customer need, being fit for purpose, with an efficient and cost-effective way of delivering it.
3. Clients are willing to pay more for products when they believe they offer a greater good for society.
4. Product innovation can be achieved by building on others' ideas or integrating products into an offering.
5. Learn by studying different industries and sectors who do similar things to you and home in on the business models of successful competitors.
6. Selecting the right suppliers is important to ensure you deliver on customer promises, so consider them as part of your team.
7. Check suppliers' past performance on reputation, capability, service consistency, financial sustainability, reliability and positive relationships.
8. Brand congruency is the unwavering commitment to consistent behaviour, quality and professionalism.
9. Great customer service can be measured at all stages of the client interaction touch points.
10. Customers do not make buying decisions based on price, but on the emotional connection they feel.

[1] http://news.cnet.com/Good-for-business,-good-for-society/2008-1036_3-6212067.html

[2] *Patagonia, the Footprint Chronicles.* http://www.patagonia.com/us/footprint/

[3] Sisodia, R., Wolfe, D., Sheth, J. (2007). *Firms of Endearment: How World-Class Companies Profit from Passion and Purpose*, Pearson Prentice Hall.

[4] Walt Disney Mission Statement. http://retailindustry.about.com/od/retailbestpractices/ig/Company-Mission-Statements/Walt-Disney-Mission-Statement.htm

[5] The Chartered Institute of Marketing. http://www.camfoundation.com/PDF/Cost-of-customer-acquisition-vs-customer-retention.pdf

[6] Antonio Damasio on the Relationship between Emotions and Decision Making. http://aarronwalter.com/2010/11/27/antonio-damasio-on-the-relationship-between-emotion-and-decision-making/

Chapter 10

Creating and Implementing Strategy

OVERVIEW

- Clarity is a key requirement for individuals to best utilise their energy and for organisations to best utilise their resources.
- Every organisation requires a planning methodology which sets a high-level strategy for enabling the planning and execution of detailed implementation plans.
- High performance is the summation and integration of the systems, processes and people which, together, make a business.
- Projects are where the strategy meets implementation, and they require trained people and standardised practices to execute them.

Clarity guides the direction of any organisation. Every team member needs clarity on the way they work and the tools they have access to. Systems and processes guide behaviour, and ensure that a business can repeat its success and be consistent in its delivery, which leads to stability and sustainability.

A methodology is a framework which guides best practice and behaviours so that individuals can replicate the same outcomes each time, making the results more about the approach than an individual's own successes.

Think of the teamwork required in an aerobatic display where pilots have to fly planes in close proximity and at speed while carrying out manoeuvres in sync with each another. The experience of each pilot must be complemented with a precise knowledge of the same routines, movements and methods, and the ability to execute them in the same ways. When the team is working in complete harmony, you will not be able to associate any one plane with a specific pilot. This means the air show could be replicated regardless of who the individual pilots are. This is the ultimate aim of team performance – the ability to replicate the same service to customers in a consistent, high-quality and repeatable way.

To do this, organisations must have business systems, processes and methods that guide behaviour and set out the right way to do things, as well as how to act and respond. McDonald's is ranked as one of the best companies in the world for the quality of their business systems and processes, which are arguably the same whatever the location of their restaurants. Their success is based on their business systems.

Once a company has a good strategy, the next step is to execute it, and this stage is known as project implementation. A project can be anything from setting up a business, creating a new product, moving offices, publishing a new policy, to developing a new business process or running an event. Businesses are dependent on innovation and change, so they must embrace project management as the most sensible method to implement their strategy as effectively as possible.

Research reveals the importance of project implementation in today's highly competitive world, which requires investment in projects to deliver on results. A survey by PricewaterhouseCoopers showed that 97 per cent of respondents believe that project management is critical to business performance and organisational success, with 94 per cent agreeing that project management enables business growth.[1]

Through excellent project management, a business can best position itself at the lowest possible cost and plan to achieve consistent success. Project management has 10 key functions, or knowledge areas, that comprise scope, time, cost, quality, risk, human resources, communications, stakeholders, procurement and integration management.

Project success still needs to follow sound strategy, and strategy relies on a clear vision. When a team is brought together with shared values and a strong vision and purpose, they comprise a formidable force. In modern business, this power of purposefulness, backed by a clear direction, provides the motivation and momentum to strive for success. To drive the minds and hearts of the team means to provide them with a clear 'vision' in their head and a strong 'why' in their heart.

To tap into the 'why' that brings together passionate people, a common link must be found to a higher purpose that will ultimately give rise to a desire to serve. This brings into alignment the values they have, and the sense of good in what they are doing as a group. Synergy with shared values is unity with power. Not-for-profit organisations have tapped into this power and attract people who genuinely are passionate about the organisation's objectives and offer their time and energy to the cause, sometimes without financial reward.

While the global norm is for large organisations to exist as public companies whose shares can be traded on the stock exchange, there are some notable exceptions. Some organisations, often family-based or privately owned businesses, typically have a stronger 'why' behind their operations beyond working for short-term goals or greater profits for shareholders. The 'why' in these family businesses relates to the high desire of the individuals to continue the family tradition, to honour the family brand and the historic efforts of others, and to pass the business down to the next generation. It goes beyond making profit and has a strong focus on sustainability. In fact, sustainability is a key factor in why they exist across generations, as they are building businesses for the long term. They are building communities of people serving other people, with longevity in mind.

People in difficult situations, such as natural disasters and economic downturns, often work together with a strong emotional bond to see through the bad times with renewed commitment and determination. The production and knowledge capital remains within these companies as they weather the storm of financial uncertainty together. In other organisations that are driven by maintaining profits or perhaps have their hands tied from strict government-based employment awards that remove the flexibility of negotiating salaries down during these times, staff were laid off and companies lost.

With this family business approach there is a greater emotional connection and vested interest for the business to survive beyond just making money. Its raison d'être is to honour its founders and continue the general good that the business does in running and growing the business, providing jobs and serving its market. There is a greater purpose embedded in its very essence, and its long-term interest in sustainability over short-term profits gives it a solid foundation to build upon.

Businesses often start out with highly passionate and purposeful people as their founders, but the challenges of running the business can put out the fire of passion over time. This is often the result of not building a synergistic team that shares its vision. The passion for the business becomes hidden under the stress of running it, when sometimes all that is needed to remedy this is a sense of comradeship and someone to share the burden. A successful business needs a team. Even people who may appear to work independently, such as celebrities or other high-profile personalities in the entertainment industry, need a huge team of promoters, marketers and production people behind them. No business can operate with just one person if it is to grow, thrive and prosper. In fact, the team of individuals who run the business *are* the business. Take them out of the equation and there would be no business.

The basis of all human progress in any aspect of life is to gain clarity and then act in meaningful ways. When a leader recognises that providing clarity and communicating is their key role, the significance of planning becomes much better understood. Clarity in all the business systems and processes is important to enable standardisation and to allow the organisation to consistently deliver the same quality of experience. Remember that:

people strive for repeatable positive experiences.

The Need for Standardisation

When a business starts out it is usually dependent on a few critical people. As it grows, those people become more stretched and the team gets too big for such an intimate relationship between these key individuals. The owner's time and focus become too thinly spread over many different aspects of the business, with the result that new team members start doing things in their own way. This is when many people-related issues begin to arise and the team gets pulled in different directions. Not having any systems and processes to follow, they often introduce their own methods or they bring in parts of methodologies from their previous employment, and the business starts to lack consistency.

Without systems in place to maintain consistency, it's harder to make improvements as there is no single method being followed by the team that can be looked at collectively with a view to making it better. It becomes harder to determine if things are working because of a particular process or person, and therefore difficult to identify specific elements for improvement.

Imagine if business had four financial management systems, each managing different parts of the accounts. It would be very difficult to record and report on the overall financial position of that business. Given the need for good financial record-keeping by law, businesses usually run a single financial management system with common policies and processes in order to be able to file accurate returns. The same unified approach should be applied to all the other aspects of business. One of the greatest challenges of small businesses is that they often don't have sufficient understanding of the financial side of things, and this becomes a key contributor to the high failure rates as cash flow is critical to running a business.

Interestingly, the study of business start-ups shows that in the early stages the focus is on the founders' expertise and their relationships with their clients. As the business grows, the process becomes important as new people try to replicate the expertise of the founders. Once the process is in place, the emphasis returns to the relationships. This is why a business will grow faster when systems are developed upfront with consideration given to the people using them. When setting up a new business, it's recommended you proceed as if it were to become a franchise operation, as a franchise is based on having repeatable systems and processes, and not on one individual's expertise. Process and people are fundamentally entwined.

If the original owners of a business try to sell it later, they may find there's not a lot to sell other than their own expertise and time. The goodwill in the business is often attached directly to these individuals, which does not leave much value to be put on the business systems and process. The success of the business is still dependent on the owners and, as a result, is sometimes worthless without them. However, where a business has strong and documented systems, methodologies and processes in place, the business value is more tangible and therefore higher.

If the franchise business model is analysed, one can recognise the great benefits of having processes that are so well defined that the dependency on key personnel is obviously reduced. The process starts guiding behaviour to the point where the business is able to employ teenagers with no previous work experience and have them adding value to the business in a very short time. Each process is broken down into simple steps, with an emphasis on educational systems that place a value on the people who become part of a synergic team.

For a humanistic business, quality has three key elements: process, product and people, as defined below.

- **Process** – a humanistic business must ensure that a consistent process is followed to enable a reliable and standardised procedure at the lowest level of operations so that the methods can be improved over time.

- **Product** – a humanistic business makes sure its products meet or exceed the expectations of its customers. Product quality is a key component of an exemplary user experience, as the 'people' and environmental aspects of the user experience generally cannot overcome poor products. Loyal customers may overlook occasional non-conformances in quality, but not as an on-going experience. Loyalty can be lost if all products start underperforming over time and the high level of service they expect drops its standards.

- **People** – once good processes are in place, it is the personal charisma, manner and professionalism of the individuals involved that will add colour to the user experience. As we are all different, this can only be a guide, but staff need to be clear on the expected code of conduct and service standards, which should be in written form. They cannot act as lone rangers to the business, but use their uniqueness to add further value to an already good process.

This last element of people quality is where humanistic businesses excel. People quality is reflected not only in a person's qualifications, certifications, licences and permits, but also in their passion, professional conduct and contribution to the team synergy. People quality is what makes humanistic businesses successful and it's a difficult thing for a competitor to mimic.

A competitor can copy the process (many franchised food outlets have modelled themselves on McDonald's), and they can create similar products (there are many copycat products in the marketplace), but the people and cultural aspects are the most powerful, most complex and most difficult to understand, analyse and reproduce. The people aspects become so powerful when synergy occurs that the cumulative outcome is a strong and winning culture based on shared values, focused passion and a genuine care for the users (customers, team members, etc.). This is the brand energy that is so important in a humanistic business.

For an individual to feel part of the team, they need to feel they fit in, that their expertise is valued, that they are important, they have the resources they need and are empowered to contribute in a constructive way. Team members are like a cohesive family where support for one another is the main characteristic and everyone is contributing towards achieving a common vision.

A humanistic business tends to have a decentralised management structure, where hierarchy of positions may exist for the need of the corporate structure, but where there exists a healthy critique of current operations with the intent to continually improve. It tends to include a flexible and transparent leadership style where open questioning of management ideas helps in making more informed and purposeful decisions. This whole ethos helps in gaining the commitment of the team, better participation and a greater feeling of involvement and contribution.

Empowering team members is important to get the most out of them, but empowerment works best where there is a framework in place that they can be guided by and work within. Without any defined constraints or boundaries, empowerment may create rogue team members that may be acting to satisfy personal interests over those of the organisation.

While the people aspect is a primary focus of the humanistic business, we must recognise the contribution of the systems and processes that guide the people and their behaviours towards standardised methods of execution that can be analysed and improved over time. If we do things differently every time, we have no idea why certain projects worked and why some didn't. The justification for improvement must be evidence-based. The most important thing to understand is that a standardised process needs to exist so that in all human interactions there can be tweaks to the specific communication and engagement based on the nuances of the people involved, so the whole process can be customised to the individual customer's needs.

Take the example of a sales process. Without a defined methodology there is no means of analysing the key factors that resulted in converting a prospect to a customer. Knowing that people are either dominantly visual, auditory or kinaesthetic (feelings), each customer will have a communication preference when dealing with the salesperson. For example, in the sale of a vacuum cleaner, the visual person will tend to be interested in the colour range, the auditory person in the noise of the device, and the kinaesthetic person in the feel of the handle and motion.

The salesperson needs to follow a predefined process of introducing themselves, capturing the individual's preferences and needs and explaining the solution to their problem within the range of products, yet they must adjust their communication and engagement style to suit that of the prospective buyer. It's a combination of this set process and tweaked communication style that works most effectively. When the salesperson recognises this, they are on the path to great sales success, as their results will be more consistent. Good salespeople will advise you that they are following the company's sales process, but they are most often ignorant to the adaptive changes they naturally make to the prospective customer that are based on matching their communication styles. These are the harder skills to develop, but without the core process there is little likelihood of a consistent result.

When analysing brilliant salespeople, it's often found that their behavioural style is ideally suited to sales and deal-making (the most natural being the IS trait in the DISC model discussed in Chapter 3). They will automatically and naturally adapt to the individual's style of communication without even realising the nuances in the changes to their own delivery style.

Training must be based on process first before the nuances of personal adaptions can be explored, although most training stays at the technical process level and does not examine the personal customer service attributes that contribute to the overall user experience.

The planning framework, governance framework, information management systems and project and operational methodologies all collectively provide the foundation and stability of the business, to enable and guide the behaviours that build productive relationships. Yet the first step in the design of the business comes back to recognising the elements of clarity that must exist in the business system as a whole.

The Cycle of Clarity

Seeking clarity is a natural instinct of humans. Most people want to know about the 'how-to' in business, yet finding the 'how' comes at the end of the natural cycle of clarity. In the start-up of a business, the cycle begins with the 'what'. This effectively is the basis of what the business is offering, whether it's an IT support business, a florist, hardware store or training organisation. It's usually tied to the founder's own knowledge, expertise, interests and passions and the products and services they are capable of supplying, either themselves or through the personal networks they have access to.

Then comes the 'where', which is determined by who the target audience is and where they are. This gives clarity to the focus of the marketing strategy and the physical location and distribution channel options for the business. Ice cream shops operate best where there is a lot of foot traffic walking past as ice cream is usually an impulsive product buy, and even better located near where children are playing. Humanistic businesses choose locations, or use channels that enable them to serve the largest client base.

The 'who' relates to the people within the business (the team), the partners who are supplying products or services to the business (suppliers) and the targeted end clients (the market). All these key stakeholders form part of what a humanistic business calls users, when the user experience needs to consider each party. The individual and collective behavioural styles and shared values are the most important consideration in the selection of team members and in building a positive and synergistic team.

The 'when' then examines the timing for starting the business, bringing on new team members and releasing products and services in the market place. Some businesses thrive through bringing new innovations to the marketplace, while others comprise the second-to-market companies who leverage the market interest created by the first business, and those who come in after the 'hype' cycle when the product is in common use. Each has a different strategy and cost based on the timing, and each has a different financial outlay and revenue level. The entry point depends on the team's own expertise and strengths.

The 'how' then completes the cycle. This is where the final implementation details exist and the mechanics to putting it all together and executing the strategy. It is the detail on how to make it happen, and clearly we cannot begin the 'how' without first getting clarity on the 'what, where, who and when'. Humanistic businesses ensure that adequate processes are in place to enable the sustainability of the business. Great processes can help reduce the risk of reliance on a few key people, but ensuring that methods are in place where the key skills are made more simple through systems, procedures and guidelines, known as the intellectual property of the business. This is where the sales value is, combined with the goodwill generated in the brand energy.

The power that glues it all together and gives it strength, vibrancy and sustainability is the 'why' behind the actions of the individuals and the business. When the 'why' is strong enough, the obstacles seem smaller, and the level of energy, persistence and stamina in the team is stronger. When a business finds a strong 'why' behind what it does, it taps into the real fuel for generating great success. In fact, arguably this is the key factor that makes humanistic businesses stand out as they have a higher purpose beyond generating profits for their shareholders.

The clarity that guides an organisation's direction comes down to its planning framework, which brings together in succinct detail the strategy, and then breaks it into smaller work plans that explain its implementation. Many organisations do not define their vision or have a strategic plan, but imagine having a sports game without goalposts. All the talent on the sports field becomes useless without clarity on the direction the players have to move in, and the individual and collective energies are wasted.

It is the planning process which integrates the 'what, where, who, when, how and why' into a single succinct set of aligned documents.

A business without a plan is like a yacht without wind or a rudder, vulnerable to the ever-changing ocean current that will dictate its fate. Its destiny is more at the whim of the external environment.

The Planning Framework

All businesses are governed by their constitution or rules of association document, which is the legally binding document that sets out the purpose and objectives of the organisation. In most countries, when a business is registered, it is this document that stands as its highest legal instrument in the court of law below legislation. It often reflects the 'why' element in business terminology and explains the reasons why the business exists – in other words, the objectives.

The board of directors is the governing entity of a company or not-for-profit organisation that brings together board directors who have four key roles: setting the strategy, ensuring legislative compliance, establishing governance and selecting, appointing and evaluating the CEO. Board directors are either executive or non-executive directors. The word 'executive' simply means they have another role in the organisation, whereas 'non-executive' means they only sit on the board. For a small sole proprietor business, the owner effectively represents the board.

The board is responsible for setting the vision and strategy, and it does this through a series of documents within this framework. Where a small business does not have plans in place, it operates on the whim of the owner or market forces and therefore there may be no strategy behind its survival, stabilisation, growth or sustainability. At worst case, it needs a business plan, and often this is a requirement for a business to be eligible for loans from banks or other investors. In reality, without a plan a business is likely to grow more slowly and less progressively.

Planning frameworks require four key elements: Vision Statement, Strategic Plan, Operations Plans, and Project Plan. Together they provide total clarity to guide the organisation and every individual in it to help the business towards the board-envisaged end position. The main difference for a humanistic business is that it is driven by a higher purpose, considers the impacts on society and the environment and ensures that at each level it provides clarity to its people how their roles contribute to a common purpose, both individually and as a team.

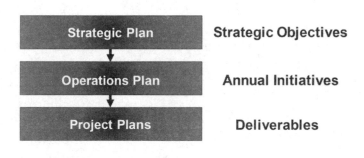

The Vision Statement

A Vision Statement sets out the envisaged end position that an organisation is looking to work towards. The statement serves two key purposes: firstly, it presents a vivid picture of the organisation's greater purpose, so that a strategy can be created for accomplishing this goal and, secondly, it taps into the emotions of the individuals in the organisation to enlist their support in following this path.

A vision statement needs to connect with the team members in order to motivate them into action and bring them together for a common purpose. In the case of a vision statement prepared for a not-for-profits organisation, it's often easier to tap into the emotions of its team members as the organisation usually exists to do meaningful social work. All organisations need to look deeper into their 'why' so they can better create a vision that demonstrates their true purpose. When there is an emotional connection to the purpose, the vision statement will be more powerful.

The vision statement primarily relates to the 'why' and 'what', and it provides clarity for establishing the rest of the strategy. Humanistic businesses often ensure their vision statement has an emotive undertone and that it represents the higher purpose of service to others. This higher purpose then guides all the work that takes place below it.

The Strategic Plan

The Strategic Plan is formulated by, or under the authority of, the board members and sets out key objectives to drive the organisation, usually within a three- or five-year period. The speed at which technology changes these days suggests a three-year duration is a smarter choice, and the reason why these plans are limited to five years maximum is that this represents the longest realistic period that team members can personally relate to. If you asked someone where they thought they would be in five years' time, they'd be able to make a calculated guess, but they would have no realistic idea if the duration were, say, 10 or more years.

Some organisations, such as environmental, power supply and water utility companies, do have to take a longer-term view as they need to consider the population growth in relation to the infrastructure they will require. However, they then have to bring it back to a five-year perspective to make it realistic for the people it guides.

Within the strategic plan are specific strategic objectives that in themselves must have clarity to be able to direct the next level of planning. The greatest failing of these objectives is when they are too ambiguous or too broad. Where there is ambiguity, there will be confusion at the lowest level of the team, the implementers. Ambiguous objectives mean that many projects could arguably be meeting the strategy, whereas the aim here is to make strategic objectives so clear that what is required from the lower level of the team is easily understood.

For example, if a business wants to grow geographically and have new offices, the board will need to specify in the strategic plan the desired countries it would like to move into, and then decisions on the exact location and operational logistics can be developed at a lower level.

The strategic plan primarily focuses on the 'what'. While a three-year plan cycle is recommended, the dynamism of some organisations today still requires the board to readdress the validity of the plan on an annual basis. A humanistic business aims to consider what is known as a balanced scorecard which looks at wider strategic areas across all the aspects of a business. This includes clients, team members, information management systems, processes, products and services, and financial stability and investment.

The Operations Plans

The annual Operations Plans, otherwise known as the Business or Tactical Plans, is linked directly to the budget. It sets out the year-by-year initiatives that will help to clarify the agenda for progressing the strategy set by the board. This level of plan is the responsibility of the executive management team or operator. When examining the multi-year operations plans side by side against the strategic plan's objectives, it gives insights into how the executive team progressed the organisation towards the board's intended strategic position each year.

In large organisations, there can be multiple operations plans that exist to set out the initiatives for each key portfolio. In this case, each portfolio determines its own priorities with regard to the strategic objectives and allocates its own sub-budget. Smaller organisations may only have one operations plan.

The aim of the operations plans is to set out a priority of the initiatives based on the total budget available and to determine the key order of importance of its investments each year. Some strategic objectives may be able to be accomplished in one year, while others may take several years of a staged roll-out implementation approach.

For example, once the board has set an objective to expand its operations into specific countries, the operations plans detail the strategy of what exactly needs to be progressed and when. The plans may create a series of initiatives, from recognising the exact location of the offices, to appointing an executive officer for each location, through to the recruitment of the team and the procurement and fit-out of those offices.

The operations plans set out broadly the 'where', 'who' and 'when'. They usually cover both on-going operational metrics, as well as new initiatives that will be implemented through programmes and projects. Programmes are simply multiple projects that need to be coordinated together. All these initiatives must align to the strategic plan to ensure the investment of time and effort is in accordance with the board's intent for growth and sustainability.

Humanistic businesses must ensure their operations plans are flexible and dynamic enough to respond to changes in the marketplace. They must consider the importance of the people and the impacts on its users. This normally means a defined change management process exists to enable a formal review and acceptance process for any proposed changes to the board-approved operations plans.

The Project Plans

The Project Plans are where the real detail exists, and these are sometimes coordinated through a programme of work where multiple projects have some common connection. The outputs of projects are called deliverables. Clarity of detail is absolutely critical here to ensure the team creates the right outputs that the project sponsor is expecting. Where there is ambiguity, there are always headaches at team level. Project plans set out not only the deliverables, but all the activities and tasks that have to be completed, together with the schedule, budget and human resource allocation. The key tool in project management to determine these is called the work breakdown structure, which forms part of the Project Management Plan (PMP).

While the deliverables set out the outputs, the work breakdown structure sets out all the work that has to be done to create those deliverables. It does this by defining the exact activities and tasks that are required to be progressed, and the schedule, budget and human resource allocation against each task. This then allows the project's progress to be tracked by following explicitly the project management plan on a day-to-day basis and monitoring the percentage completion of each task to the planned schedule and budget. During execution, risks need to be treated and issues managed.

The project management process is where the engagement and communication with the key stakeholders occurs. A project is effectively a new or unique venture where deliverables are created and delivered. They are the basis of all strategy implementation as planning involves new initiatives that need to be executed. The on-going use of the deliverables is in the operations management arena. For example, a building is constructed as a project and then occupied and maintained as an operation.

A project follows a distinct four-stage approach from concept to completion and handover into operations:

Initiation phase – this is where the project deliverables are conceptually defined and the proposed schedule and budget is calculated. The project must align with the planning framework to ensure it is a rightful investment in accordance with the organisation's overall strategy. The planning framework also considers the different ways the project could be executed. The main document it produces is most commonly called the Project Proposal, which is approved by the project sponsor. In this phase, multiple options for the project are considered and one method is ultimately proposed, together with indicative budget, schedule and human resource allocation.

Planning phase – in this phase the project deliverables are confirmed and the schedule and budget is formally agreed by the project sponsor. This is where the detailed plan that builds upon the initiation work is formalised and defines the exact process that will be followed to execute the project. The main document it produces is the project management plan (PMP) that is approved by the project sponsor. Organisations often have different project plans to cater for the different level of rigour needed for simple (minor) and complex (major) projects. The PMP will have several subsidiary plans set out as appendixes that will cover the organisational chart, work breakdown structure, schedule, budget, risk management plan, communication management plan, human resource plan, stakeholder plan and procurement plan. Once approved it becomes the work plan for execution.

Execution phase – this is where the project deliverables are created and the work breakdown structure is followed until all the project tasks are completed. During the execution phase, meetings are conducted with agendas produced and minutes recorded; changes are formally managed through a change or variation management process;

inspections, tests and audits are validated through quality variation reports; risks and issues are tracked and dealt with; and monthly progress is reported. Each task set out in the work breakdown is tracked by percentage complete that is referred to as earned value management, and compared to the plan to enable the management of the project to be delivered on time, within budget and to the predefined deliverable specification. This allows you to track the actual progress against the planned progress, alerting the team to delays or negative trends. Once all the deliverables are created to their predefined quality specifications, the phase is completed.

Close-out phase – in this final phase the project deliverables are handed over to the project sponsor, lessons learnt are recorded, the team is disbanded, all payments are made and the project is formally closed by the project sponsor signing the Close-out Report. All documentation is then archived. Closure is done in two parts: administration close-out and contract close-out, recognising the basic project elements must still be finalised even though legal issues may stay open until resolved at a later date.

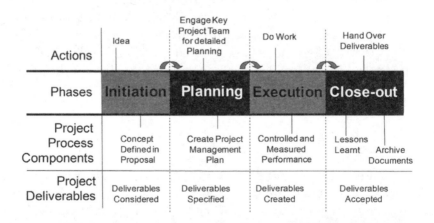

Actions	Idea	Engage Key Project Team for detailed Planning	Do Work	Hand Over Deliverables
Phases	**Initiation**	**Planning**	**Execution**	**Close-out**
Project Process Components	Concept Defined in Proposal	Create Project Management Plan	Controlled and Measured Performance	Lessons Learnt Archive Documents
Project Deliverables	Deliverables Considered	Deliverables Specified	Deliverables Created	Deliverables Accepted

In reviewing the high-performing organisations that are running projects successfully, the Project Management Institute, which is the global professional association for the project management profession, has concluded that there are three key focus areas for businesses: talent management (recognising the importance of the people involved in the projects and the needs for project skills), standardisation (the need for a project management framework that guides behaviour) and alignment with strategy (the need for projects to align with the organisation's strategic direction).

Business is all about people, and so too are projects. In fact, global research into project failures almost exclusively concludes that it is the people factors that cause projects to fail. From a humanistic business perspective, this means identifying and engaging with key stakeholders that are involved or impacted by the project and have the ability to influence it.

It also requires having a framework that guides good behaviour, and this is most commonly referred to as a project management methodology. An example of a project management is demonstrated in the Project Rite™ Methodology, which portrays all the potential templates and registers required for a complex project:

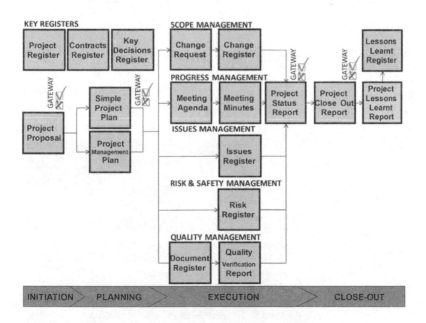

As projects are the mechanisms for execution strategy, every organisation should ensure that the key project management methodology components exist for comparison and improvement purposes.

A humanistic business recognises that when there is a framework in place that guides good behaviour, team members are best informed and supported, and that such resources assist in providing the standardised approaches. The methodology takes care of the process, so the team can focus on the people and technical issues that come with change. Projects cover all aspects of the business, from starting the business, to relocating its offices, through to creating new products and implementing new services.

When businesses use project documentation, they start capturing corporate information and lessons from their experiences to feed back into future projects. This allows the organisation to grow, to evolve and to avoid planning from scratch each time instead of building on practices that have already shown their worth. While a project management methodology enables best practice in project management, the need for standardisation applies across all facets of the business.

Clarity Across the Business

In addition to the planning framework which defines the strategy and the follow-on implementation plans for that strategy, there are seven key areas for additional clarity that the leadership of a humanistic business needs to provide:

1. Policies and Procedures
2. Organisational Structure
3. Information Management Systems
4. Target Market
5. Products and Services
6. Team Functional Roles
7. Individual Roles

These are explained as:

- **Policies and Procedures** (What and Where) – this represents the governing and guiding documents which help define the appropriate and professional behaviours expected of team members.

- **Organisational Structure** (internal Who) – this represents the functional structure and hierarchy of authority. It's important to ensure clear authority and a structure to the functions that makes sense and offer defined responsibility at all levels.

- **Information Management Systems** (What, Who and How) – this represents the information management systems that guide and often enforce specific practices, including record-keeping and legislative compliance. These systems must help make the tasks easier, and their security and access should be aligned with the roles, so that who can access, use and modify the information is well known. Information management systems also guide behaviour from a technology perspective.

- **Target Market** (Who, Where and When) – this represents the particular target customers and demographic information that enables the team to be purposeful and specific in their marketing to those whom the business is primarily focused to serve.

- **Team Functional Roles** (Who, Where and What) – this represents the information of the hierarchical organisational structure and the team's function, role and responsibilities. It enables the team to be clear on how the organisation is structured and to know what is expected of them as a group.

- **Individual Roles** (Who, What and How) – this represents the specific role, responsibilities and authorities of individuals, and their area of contribution, which enables each team member to be purposeful in their own work.

People want clarity and they want to feel important. When they have a task for which they are responsible, they require clarity about their individual and team role, and they want to know how they add value and what is expected of them, so they can have the right elements in place for high performance. The final key element relies on the under-pinning 'why' and the synergy between the individuals that makes them work together as a team. This synergy of the team beyond their individual roles and responsibilities is derived from shared values, clear communications and compatible behavioural styles. This is why humanistic businesses strive to influence the team dynamics.

The design of the business systems and processes provides the tangible intellectual property which helps increase the value of the business should it be up for sale. More importantly, in operating the business, these guiding systems and processes are what ultimately influence the culture and brand energy to be able to continue beyond the contributions of the key founding people who began the business.

Independent of good process, people still run the systems and have a strong influence on the brand energy. A new CEO can reverse the great work of the previous leader. Good brand energy can start to dissipate and, at worst case, die. Brand reputation can be destroyed fast. Recognise that great process guides good behaviour and, without these systems and processes, there is an even higher risk of business success being solely dependent on a few key people who could be gone tomorrow.

Key Lessons

1. Create clarity by defining individual and organisational purpose, values and goals.

2. The cycle of clarity comprises knowing the 'what, where, who, when and how', and giving it the power of the 'why'.

3. Organisations must start their operations with a high moral purpose and remain loyal to it throughout.

4. Match personal and organisational values that are driven by purpose and passion and the organisation will attract excited and loyal staff who will stick with it and become the organisation's greatest innovators and assets.

5. Link effort to reward. People need to know that they make a difference and will be remunerated in a system that is transparent, fair and related to performance.

6. Consciously integrate enjoyment, engagement and meaning, to produce a culture of happiness.

7. It is the responsibility of the organisation to create an environment and culture that nurtures and develops individual's natural gifts so each individual can become a high performer.

8. In a humanistic business, senior levels of management must provide clarity on objectives and purpose through all levels of the organisation.

9. Peak performance is based upon an internal reference, one that is related to personal values and aligned with the leveraging of natural potential.

10. Consistent results are an integration of great process and great people. Process guides behaviour.

11. The ultimate objective is happiness for all internal and external stakeholders.

---

[1] PWC (2012). Insights and Trends: Current Portfolio, Programme and Project Management Practices, The Third Global Survey on the Current State of Project Management, PriceWaterhouseCoopers, http://www.pwc.com/en_US/us/public-sector/assets/pwc-global-project-management-report-2012.pdf, accessed 22 November 2013.

Chapter 11

Creating Brand Power

OVERVIEW

- A positive emotional response in people is the key driver for branding.
- Brand power is the life force and differentiation strategy for a business, and is reflected in the brand awareness in the marketplace, the emotional response to the brand name and the culture of the organisation.
- Branding needs to be protected, nurtured and strategically managed to represent the image desired.
- Brand power is not created by what the business says it does, but by what it actually does and how that message and the products are accepted by the marketplace.
- Colours have meanings, and the design of the corporate logo as well as the colour schemes used in the packaging of products and office decor are important.

When profit remains the only driving force behind an organisation's actions and strategic planning, its values and purpose can be compromised. This is where its brand energy and power begin a slow death and the organisation eventually becomes unsustainable. People buy because of emotional engagement. Betray the purpose and values the organisation stands for, and the business ultimately betrays the customer. Success is directly linked to the emotional connection between the organisation and its key stakeholders. This emotional connection is the brand energy that the humanistic model delivers.

An organisation's brand is not just the logo or trade name, nor its corporate colours or the slogans they promote. It is not the strategy it follows, or the business systems it operates. It goes beyond all these tangible things, to become the essence of what the business represents. This essence is communicated throughout the values, culture and behaviour of the organisation and is projected into the outside world in the same way a person might project their reputation.

Branding starts with a trade name, then a logo and the forming of a business with its people, products and services. It begins as a thought, a concept and a potential.

Brand is the one element that cannot be so easily copied, mimicked or stolen from another organisation and is a direct result of its underlying culture. It goes beyond the products and services, beyond individuals, beyond marketing strategies and into the realm of representing a living entity. As such, it needs nourishment, nurturing and social interaction that gives the organisation its personality and presence. This presence also extends beyond the incumbent management to each and every team member. It can be likened to nurturing a child that will outlive the parent and go on to experience things that the parents will not, engendering a sense of responsibility in the next generation. This implies that the management of a brand is more of a stewardship role than one of ownership.

Brand energy is almost unexplainable, yet its existence is proven through loyal customers, advocates talking about the business, its ability to sell products and services and its attractiveness to people. It did not exist before the business, yet it was like a seed that formed into a tree, following a process of evolution. Its importance is directly linked to its ability to create business following the principle that:

strong positive brand energy attracts people.

To understand the phenomenon of brand power is to recognise there is a three-phase evolution at play. The first is the inception, then the proposition that relates to the market engagement and finally the market recognition.

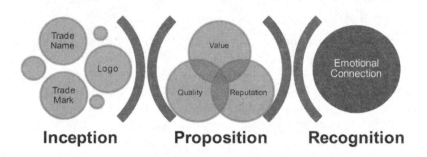

Inception   Proposition   Recognition

At its inception it starts as a concept that leads to the tangible brand name, logo and sometimes a trademark. Through its people, products and services, it goes to market offering value, quality and a projected reputation that is driven by the business as part of its outward market proposition. Through the relationships between the people in the organisation and their key stakeholders, it begins to form a reputation with the external key stakeholders who start to recognise the brand and associate it with an emotion. When this emotion is positive, it means the brand has gained market positioning and power. The higher the awareness of the brand, the greater its power. In fact, brand energy has a value that accountants call goodwill. Each of these individual and cumulative elements needs to be examined to identify the steps involved in creating this power.

Inception Phase

This phase is where clarity is established on the structural, legal and symbolic elements of defining the business in a marketable format that will be presented and promoted in the marketplace. This includes the name of the business, and the legal structure it exists within, from its board members, owners and operators, right through to the symbolism in its logo, the corporate colours it portrays and the intellectual property protection it holds in the form of trademarks, images, designs and trade names.

Brand name

There are many different approaches to creating a business name, also referred to as a trade name. A single business can have only one legal name, but it may have multiple trade names under which it conducts its business. Using multiple trade names can be detrimental by causing market confusion, although sometimes it may be beneficial if it helps to better represent an offering to a specific market segment, or it can be used under licence to link it to another entity, such as a franchise. A trade name ideally needs to be one where you have control of the domain name, as your online presence is an important marketing factor.

A short name has fewer words for the customer to remember (e.g. eBay, Google, LinkedIn, Apple, Wal-Mart, IBM). If the business name uses a known word in the dictionary, then it may be more difficult to trademark it, and trademarks are the highest legal protection for a name or logo. If using a combination of known words, it's often smart to use words that help to define what the business does. Creating new words avoids the challenge of having issues with trademarks and domain names, but they may cause confusion unless a person is able to spell the name correctly after listening to it. This spelling challenge becomes problematic for Internet searches, and many domain names have been secured by companies using the most likely typing errors for another competitor's business's name, to allow them to capture the search of a potential prospect.

Some industries, such as law and accounting, use the founder's name. However, using the owner's name for small businesses may suggest a one-person operation, which could be less attractive to some potential customers. More importantly, a business that uses the founder's name could be harder to sell in the future as the owner would have to allow others to operate under their personal brand.

Following the principle of 'being easy to do business with', the best names are short, able to be trademarked, unique and memorable.

Logo designs

A logo may include an image that represents the business, sometimes combined with the business's name, acronym or other phrase. The design of a logo should take into account the emotional effect it will have on other people and whether the design needs to fit with the desired level of professionalism. For instance, a home-based business logo will usually look different to a corporate logo.

The most important consideration is the choice of colour or colours, as each colour has its own significance:

- **Blue** – represents trustworthiness, dependability and commitment. Following the colour of the sky and the ocean, blue is perceived as a constant in our lives. It can represent peacefulness and calm, and is the least gender-specific colour as it has equal appeal to both men and women. It is the most favoured colour and appeals to all ages and genders.

- **Green** – represents renewal, self-control, relaxation and harmony. The natural greens in plants are seen as tranquil and refreshing, and can provide a sense of connection to nature.

- **Yellow (Gold)** – represents optimism, enlightenment and happiness. Shades of golden yellow carry the promise of a positive future, success and wealth. Yellow instils optimism and energy.

- **Orange** – represents fun, flamboyance, warmth, social inclusion and energy. People tend to either love or hate this colour and so its appeal is limiting, although its lighter terracotta and peach hues tend to have a broader appeal.

- **Red** – represents enthusiasm, energy, action, confidence, strength and excitement. It can have connections with the extremities of love and hate and is therefore a very emotive colour.

- **Purple** – represents royalty, leadership and mysticism. It is uplifting and often associated with spirituality. It presents a sense of power and authority and yet steadiness and strength.

- **Brown** – represents stability, reliability and approachability. It symbolises the earth and can be associated with nature. It also offers a sense of orderliness. Brown is not used much in logos as the colour does not merge well with others.

- **Grey (Silver)** – represents practicality, reliability, stability and predictability. It may also be linked to loss and wisdom. Silver is a precious metal that is associated with financial security.

- **White** – represents purity, cleanliness and neutrality. It has a sense of openness, and new beginnings. White light is the synthesis of colours.

- **Black** – represents authority, possibility and power. It can carry a sense of the mystic, unknown and emptiness. It is often argued that black light is not a colour, as being opposite to white, it is the absence of colour. This is because in the absence of light, darkness makes everything appear black.

The selection of colours has an important subconscious connection with people, and logos that blend colours, including their hues and saturations, need to consider the messages being conveyed. Humanistic businesses are best served with trusting, reliable and optimistic colours.

Trademarks

A trademark offers the highest level of legal protection for a trade name, design or logo. Trademarks are registered in the country of origin. However, they can be registered in multiple countries or through cross-country agreements like the Madrid Protocol. A trademark is a sign of ownership, and for a name to qualify as a trademark, it will either need to be identifiably unique or distinctive, or proven to be distinctive because of its long-term trading use by the organisation concerned.

Trademarks can either be registered, meaning they have been formally recognised by a government regulator, or unregistered, meaning that an organisation is declaring its name to be a trademark without the formal registration. Trademark types are declared by use of symbols, such as the ® that stands for registered. Many trade names or phrases can be declared unregistered trademarks by adding a symbol that may be recognised by certain countries or jurisdictions, such as the ™ mark.

Coca-Cola used an unregistered trademark for years because they had a strong legal argument that it was their rightful unregistered trademark, but once it became registered by an authority, it carried a stronger legal weight. The challenge with any form of trademark protection is that the owner must action and pay for the legal costs to protect it, meaning that in any breaches of their trademark, the law requires them to take action against the perpetrator.

Trademark authority does not automatically define ownership, unlike the ownership of a domain name, but can control the use of the trademark. In this case, the use of a domain name can be stopped when trademark rights apply, subject to any challenge to the geographic-based registration limits of the trademark.

Proposition Phase

In this phase the marketplace is engaged, rapport is built and trade enjoyed. It is where the business starts to serve others and stabilises itself through income, and where the brand is connected to the delivery of products and services, and their quality levels. The reason why it's called the proposition phase is because the brand's success is based on its clients' perceptions and not just on the marketing face the business thinks it projects.

This is the brand in action in the marketplace, and the trust it builds from it being fit for purpose, and from its reliability, consistency and the value of the organisation's offerings. This trust extends to warranties, guarantees and living up to those promises. The brand's awareness and market share is important, and whether the business is deemed a leader or follower in the industry are all positioning factors.

The value proposition is the offer to the marketplace that represents the benefits of its products and services. Humanistic businesses strive to present high value not only to their customers, but also to the wider key stakeholders. Value can be both tangible and intangible. When creating the value a business presents to the market, it extends to the user experience, the way the team serves their clients and how it engages and enhances society.

As defined earlier, the quality attributes of a business have three dimensions, comprising the quality of the *product,* based on its specification and functionality; quality in the *process,* represented by the systems and processes offering consistent and repeatable results, which is important for building confidence in clients; and *people* quality, represented by the professionalism and attitudes of the team in building rapport with clients, as well as the qualifications, licences and permits they possess in order to meet the legislative requirements to operate.

The quality attributes of a humanistic business are one of the most important characteristics of standout businesses. They create a sense of reliability, stability, trustworthiness and predictability that are vital for connecting to a wider market and getting the market talking about a business's offerings. These are applied to the user experience to enable repeatable positive experiences that become the norm when dealing with the business.

Finally, the position of the business relates to whether it creates the dynamics as a market leader, market follower or whether its other attributes make it the preferred supplier among its competitors.

Building a strong reputation takes time, yet it can be taken away in minutes. The governing framework, systems and processes are essential for guiding professional behaviours, and for recruiting, inducting, training and developing team members to engage with others in a professional, ethical and values-aligned way.

As well as positioning for market share, position can include the geographic location, number of offices, distribution channels, partnerships and alliances, all of which effectively relate to the way stakeholders are engaged.

Reputation Phase

The reputation phase considers a feedback loop from the marketplace as to the performance and acknowledgement of the business's value and position. It is the external check on how the outside world recognises the business, which is referred to as its public reputation.

The positioning in the marketplace is created by two primary factors: what the business presents to the marketplace that one has control over, including the internal view of the business that represents the proposition; and how the market relates and responds. Based upon the response that is received, reputation is established.

The true basis of a solid reputation in the marketplace is when a business has achieved great success indirectly linking to the emotional connection between the organisation and its key stakeholders. Many successful businesses that are not humanistic often lose market share to competitors who have established a positive emotional connection between themselves and the customers. This essential element of a humanistic business is largely created by a focus on creating exemplary user experiences.

These elements provide a roadmap for focusing on areas of business performance, and using the loop between the proposition and reputation phases as a 'do and review' cycle that presents a process improvement feedback loop. When the cycle is examined the starting point is the point of execution (delivery), and then both the internal (review) and external (feedback) input is critically analysed which leads to improvement (updates) that are then fed back into the systems, processes and expected team behaviours. This is why the proposition and reputation phases are in a continuous loop.

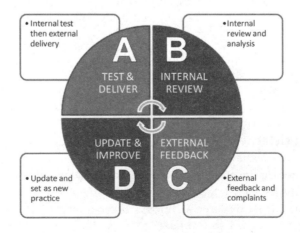

Having mechanisms to capture authentic and comprehensive team and customer feedback is critical when looking for areas to improve. This way, process improvements act as a guide to improve professional behaviour toward creating better results.

Such feedback may be in many forms, such as surveys, assessments, feedback slips, improvement tips, grievances, complaints, website analytics, awards, audits and lessons learnt. The aim is to gain honest feedback that is accepted as key lessons for indicating areas for improvement. It follows the same philosophy of life-learning that we can always continue to do things better and that we are always open to new ideas and willing to learn and change.

Creating a Winning Culture

When looking at the elements that feed into brand power, the key difference in a humanistic business is that it has team members with shared values who are well aligned with the organisation's purpose and are committed to its strategic direction. The products and services it offers can be similar to those offered by other organisations, but it is the culture that makes it so unique.

Cultures cannot be bought, and are not a tangible element that can be simply plugged into the organisation like a management system. Culture is created by a set of shared assumptions that directs how an organisation defines aligned or misaligned behaviour. The greatest challenge for evolving organisations is to align the collective values, beliefs, language and emotions of their teams and create emotional engagement that brings the diversity of perspectives into a powerful brand force. It is the hardest element of a business to understand, to study, to research and to analyse, but it is the most important element of all. It is the lifeblood of the organisation and the very element that gives the business its uniqueness. The commitment of the organisation to invest in the personal and professional evolution of its staff is perhaps the best investment in developing a sustainable humanistic culture that creates enthused advocates of the brand.

Brand energy, and the market power it offers, is another way of describing the outcome of a great culture. It's not just about people, as there needs to be a tangible output in the form of products or services that bring together the value and benefits.

The humanistic culture is heavily influenced by people, and the key elements that were found to be part of guiding the culture were largely attributable to providing clarity and making people feel important. They included purpose, autonomy, values alignment and engagement ethos.

Purpose

Human beings need to know where they fit and how they can contribute. There is much research that demonstrates a mismatch between what science now knows and what many businesses do. Motivating individuals with extrinsic rewards such as money, doesn't always work in the way we expect. The exception is where the work is of low variety, low identity and low significance, underpinned typically with a set of defined rules with a clear destination and extrinsic financial rewards. In these cases, money does seem to be a significant motivating factor, as the internal connection to our values is not engaged. However, much of our work these days is complex in nature, the rules are often flexible or ill-defined and the destination is not always clear when we start.

For activities like this, intrinsic motivation has proved to be a much better approach for engaging people and providing a sense of achievement and purpose. Businesses need to have a very clear sense of purpose, and everything that individuals within the organisation do should demonstrate some direct contribution towards this purpose. Walt Disney's aim was simply 'to make people happy', Google describe theirs as 'to organise the world's information and make it universally accessible and useful'. People are 'purpose maximisers' and the more they feel connected to something that is bigger than themselves and are making a direct contribution towards it, the more motivated they will be. Business and technology author Daniel Pink says: 'When the profit motive becomes unmoored from the purpose motive, bad things happen.'[1] He believes that if there is a disconnect between these two things, then customer service becomes poor or apathetic, and product development and delivery suffers.

Autonomy

If compliance is desired, tell people what to do, but if engagement is the goal, then allow them to be self-directed, responsible and autonomous. People are often surprised about how human beings behave when given the opportunity to express their skills and creativity. Remember the traffic-calming experiment of woonerfs we discussed in Chapter 3, and how through the process of removing the rules, drivers and pedestrians changed their mind-set by raising their awareness, which resulted in their behaving more responsibly. The Australian software company Atlassian has a Ship It day once every quarter, where employees are allowed to work on anything that relates to their products and with whomever they want. The only rule is that they must deliver their result at the end of the 24-hour period. The company says it fosters creativity, allows people to get radical and also have fun and it results in some great product features. Google, Facebook, LinkedIn and Apple have reportedly done the same. Google established a policy based on allocating 20 per cent of the team's time to experimenting with their own ideas.

In Google's Project Oxygen,[2] which aimed to make engineers better managers, the company looked back over all their performance reviews, feedback surveys and award nominations and generated a list of key management practices, in order of importance. The first of these was 'be a good coach', which related to providing specific, constructive feedback. The second was to 'empower your team and don't micromanage'. It advises managers to 'balance giving freedom to your employees, while still being available for advice. Make "stretch" assignments to help the team tackle big problems.'

If the right people were recruited, then the organisation's job becomes about creating the right environment, supported by the most appropriate leadership style and to present opportunities to bring out the best in those people.

Values alignment

When recruiting team members, it's important to choose people whose values align with those of the organisation, and who demonstrate personal integrity. The more purpose-driven and autonomous a culture, the more the leaders will require the skills to operate within a non-hierarchical and much more flexible framework, compared with traditional business models. Google recognised the importance of this in their Project Oxygen research, and as well as identifying the key good behaviours of managers they also identified pitfalls for leading people within their culture, reporting that: 'Sometimes, fantastic individual contributors are promoted to managers without the necessary skills to lead people . . . People hired from outside the organisation don't always understand the unique aspects of managing at Google.'[3] This alignment of values and matching of skills and personal qualities with organisational culture is an important factor.

Not-for-profit organisations do it well because the purpose of the organisation is what attracts the individuals in the first place. Often the team members suffer from low pay and poor conditions, but are rewarded through the sense of doing a noble thing and contributing back to the society in some form that is totally aligned with their values.

Remember, companies hire on talent, but fire on misaligned values. The key challenge is being able to access values during the recruitment process, and to weight its importance as part of the decision for employing people.

Engagement ethos

The internal cultural aspects of any organisation set the tone for any outward-looking engagements, such as relationships with customers and suppliers. The John Lewis Partnership suggests that integrity and courtesy characterise their relationships with any external groups and that they set out to honour scrupulously every business agreement they make.[4] This sense of authenticity and integrity should run through everything a humanistic business does and, because of its visibility, become the overriding factor that will influence and define brand power.

By securing trust as well as providing outstanding choice, value and service, it's possible to build loyalty similar to that experienced by sports teams. The emotional connection people make becomes the differentiator and provides robustness through challenging times and sustainability over the long term.

Making a Brand Powerful

A logo has power in itself, engaging the emotions through its colour, symbolism and style, but its energy is what the prospect and customer have come to associate this logo with. The brand power is the market energy created in representing a business, its people, its products and its services, and the outward results and contributions it makes to society. Brand energy is the culture and its expression.

A humanistic business brings something far beyond the assumptions that are in its products. A cup of coffee is not just a cup of coffee when you consider where you bought it from. As Howard Schultz of Starbucks says:

> *'Mass advertising can help build brands, but authenticity is what makes them last. If people believe they share values with a company, they will stay loyal to the brand.'*[5]

Purposeful emotional connection is what business is all about, and it is people who generate the emotional element that creates and sustains brand power. This brand power is reflected in the organisation's culture and it is a business's greatest differentiation in the marketplace.

Key Lessons

1. Brand strength is the emotional buy-in of all stakeholders and follows a three-step evolutional sequence. First is inception, leading to proposition which relates to market engagement and market recognition.
2. When designing your business logo, remember colour has meaning at a subconscious level and affects the emotional response in the general public.
3. Quality is a major characteristic of a humanistic business because it creates reliability, stability, trustworthiness and predictability, which result in a repeatable positive experience for the customers.
4. For sustainable success, a feedback loop from customers must include a measure of performance and product or service delivery which is used to improve the customer engagement. This builds reputation vital to the brand distinction.

5. Success is directly linked to the emotional connection between the organisation and its key stakeholders.
6. Culture is the lifeblood of an humanistic organisation. It's the very element that creates a uniqueness to the brand that can't be copied by the competition.
7. When the collective values, beliefs, language and emotions of a team are aligned, you have emotional engagement, which brings diverse perspectives into a powerful brand force.
8. When an organisation's purpose is pushed aside for profit at all cost, then the culture and brand begins to slowly deteriorate.

[1] Pink, D. RSA Animate – Drive – The surprising truth about what motivates us. http://www.youtube.com/watch?v=u6XAPnuFjJc

[2] http://www.nytimes.com/2011/03/13/business/13hire.html?pagewanted=all&_r=0

[3] Ibid.

[4] http://www.johnlewispartnership.co.uk/about/our-principles.html

[5] Schultz, H. (1997). *Pour Your Heart Into It: How Starbucks Built a Company One Cup at a Time*, Hyperion.

Chapter 12

Designing the User Experience

OVERVIEW

- The user experience represents the holistic emotional response as a result of engaging with the business.
- Users are defined not only as the customers or prospects, but also the staff, suppliers, investors, board directors, government and society.
- Touch points are events of interaction between the business and the prospect or client, and include both human and non-human interactions.
- Touch points can be measured by their emotional quotient.
- Touch points and the customer user experience can be designed, role-played and improved over time.
- Stakeholder feedback is critical to the improvement process.

Designing the business through adequate planning, executing, monitoring and adjusting are all key parts for any business to evolve. A business can be run in a reactive and unplanned manner or as a calculated strategy that maximises the relationship with the customer. The reality is that without concerted effort in design, the business will be less able to respond positively and flexibly to changing market conditions or stakeholder expectations.

Design brings together strategy, evolution and innovation. Human DNA is made up of chemical building blocks which offer biological instructions needed for us to develop, survive and reproduce. Similarly, the building blocks in business DNA provides instructions for enabling consistent and continually improving processes that guide the team's behaviours.

The user experience is the expression of the business DNA. It is a primary focus and differentiator of the humanistic business. The term 'user' extends beyond just customers, and includes investors, team members, suppliers, government and society. This DNA is a reflection of who we are and what our business represents. It must ensure an enjoyable interaction with each user group to create and sustain a positive emotional response that encourages continued engagement.

User touch points represent an intersection of a communication between a stakeholder and the business through its team members. Touch points, such as electronic newsletters, enable a business to maintain a profile and relationship with its users on a regular basis. The aim is to create frequent positive touch points that enable the business to maintain its reputation in offering value, such as the publication of YouTube clips, eBooks or articles which are usually free to the clients or part of a membership service. Touch points that add value build trust. This is why many businesses are now looking at ways to provide free value online in the hope of building trusted and strong relationships that ultimately lead to income. When a person enjoys and sees the value in content being provided free, there's a point where the business may make an offer of a related product. The client is now confident that this product is something of value to them, or they simply want more of what they have already been exposed to. This is the concept of upselling through showing value and building the relationship over time, and then pitching another level of transaction or engagement. This process also aims to create credibility, likeability, reputation and trust in the business.

Our interactions with customers do not have to be surprises. In fact, they can often be predicted when based on delivering a consistent customer service approach. This means the business needs to take control of those factors that can lead to a positive interaction. More importantly, we know that repeatable positive interactions are what people want. This explains why travellers may still favour buying food or beverages through their recognisable franchise-branded suppliers. There is a higher expectation of predictability and consistency. This is why it's important to design the conditions for a consistent positive experience through the team members' actions during these interactions.

Each touch point is an event' that can be studied. These events, in sequence, lead to an overall user experience. Where trust has been built and value recognised, there is a positive connection between the client or prospect and the business. By creating an exceptional and positive user experience, staff are retained, loyal customers are grown and suppliers are attracted. The aim is to create the right environment so that people want to be engaged with the business. Customers are willing to refer other people, team members are proud to promote the organisation outside of normal business hours and suppliers are proud of their association with the brand and use it as an example when speaking with others. This sense of pride and connection is the outcome of the business's DNA.

The objective of an exemplary user experience is for the business and its brand to become what the customer wants to be associated with. It explains why someone selects a particular coffee shop over another, or a specific supplier over another. It's why certain trade names trigger confidence within the customer over time, and why brand association is important in partnerships and alliances. Even a simple corporate logo can result in an emotional response that can be instantly recognised among the many competing sensory inputs we are receiving every second. It also explains why customer loyalty can be created through the business being perceived as doing good in the world. These things may include the way the business manages its waste, uses recyclable products and avoids animal testing, or it may be the charitable work the business is involved in. Basically it is a reflection of the inherent nature that the business has come to be known for. This is the essence of a business's DNA.

A new business can begin with a planned user experience strategy even before it opens its doors for trade. Existing businesses have the opportunity to review, analyse and identify what it is currently doing and how it can improve. Every organisation needs to benchmark how it does things today so it can evolve and track that development to help it find a better way of doing business tomorrow. This process is called the 'user experience emotional analysis'.

This process starts by applying a mystery-shopper approach where the analyst masquerades as a client. Each touch point is recorded, whether it be a phone call, email, sms, letter or face-to-face interaction with the business. The analyst captures these events, recording the date, time and detail of the interaction. These statistics provide insights to key elements of each specific event that are then mapped against the emotional experience of the analyst who represents the pseudo client. This is plotted on what is called an 'emotional map' graph.

The emotional map represents multiple emotional states, from extreme positive to extreme negative. Coupled with the event detail, the experience can be examined to determine what emotional response the team member or business environment evoked in the client.

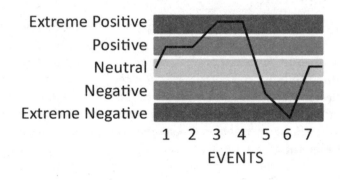

The plotting of the emotional map and the key factors that impact a client's emotional state become obvious in analysis of the process. More importantly, the touch point detail gives an absolute insight into the causes of the emotional effect. This provides a clear picture of those parts of the business interactions that are working effectively, as well as identifying what needs to be adjusted or changed.

A team member interaction should also include any automated process, such as an automatic email message that confirms receipt of an electronic email, or an auto-generated help desk number given to the client to track an issue they have reported. These interactions should be considered as a human-replaced interaction that still needs to be analysed. The importance of this is that a client receiving a voice recording rather than actually speaking to a person will evoke a different emotional response, so in tracking the event detail, you come to see if business automation is helping or inhibiting the client's user experience.

There are many examples of outsourced help desks from overseas companies where the language differences cause communication issues that then reflect poorly in the customer service satisfaction surveys. Equally, there are automated processes that cause frustration. Consider the automated phone messages that require you to type a specific number into the keypad. If the keypad is not sending out recognisable messages, the client has no way of bypassing or progressing the inputting of the number.

Client frustration is only one perspective, as team members will also have their own related concerns. Many people get frustrated by the automatic process of having to enter an account or PIN number during a robotic automation only to be transferred to a real person who asks for the same information. Often the team member who is asking for the information does not have access to the electronic data that has been collected. They know the client is likely to complain and there is little they can do about it as the issue is with the application of the technology. They grin and bear it, while the customer remains unsatisfied and frustrated.

The fundamental aim of process improvement is to make it as easy as possible for customers to do business with the company. This means each stage of the process must represent an efficient and positive step towards the desired outcome, such as fewer clicks on a website to achieve the same result. For example, when people are buying products online some systems request the completion of certain fields, which is a smart technique to make sure mandatory information is captured and checked. We've all had the experience where some of these systems do not provide all the right options to enable the progress of the transaction, such as a dropdown menu that does not include the country where the client is transacting from. They become locked out of progressing the transaction, the income is lost and the client leaves frustrated and potentially highly motivated to complain about the service. In an age where public comments on sites such as Facebook or TripAdvisor can directly and easily impact a business's reputation, this is a situation to be avoided.

When the user-experience-emotional-analysis approach is used in testing technology, the test is more about the emotional state that the technology is influencing, rather than the business process itself. Combining a positive emotional response with an efficient process creates a win-win outcome that enhances the way your business interacts with its users.

The aim of this user experience emotional analysis is to:

- enable a traceable validation of an interactive process between a team member or automated business process and a client within a defined timeline;
- enable the analysis of the journey against expected service standards, which provides a quantitative measure of what the client is receiving over the business's intent;
- capture what in the process was beneficial and what was detrimental to relationship-building, based on the recording of the qualitative measure of the emotion response of the client from each event touch point; and
- make recommendations on what could have been done differently to improve the user experience and thereby improve the process.

The analysis is a record of emotions against touch point events. Each event is captured in detail in the report, and the extra depth of information is aligned with the corresponding recorded emotional state in order to compare mechanical responses to emotional intelligence responses.

The challenge comes from the fact that some clients will simply never complain or provide any feedback. Their disinterest is only noticeable from the fact that they never return as a client, and if there is no means of monitoring this, the organisation remains ignorant of the reason for the loss. Take the example of a bad meal at a restaurant: only a few people will notify the staff of their dissatisfaction, while others will hold their opinions and never be seen again. Businesses need to address all opportunities for feedback and use the user experience analysis process to get greater insights into the reality of what is actually happening and why.

When the pseudo client engages in a touch point, they record the time of day, the people involved and information about the nature of the interaction. This becomes useful content to compare to their personal emotional experience to see why their responses change. The business is effectively questioning each element and what makes for a good experience and what disengages, frustrates or upsets the client. On later analysis, the event can be compared to the documented service standards to ensure the team members were acting in accordance with the business policies and procedures that are there to enable consistent measures over time. Too often these standards are not being met, and this process highlights those occasions.

Interestingly, when behaviour is analysed and any non-compliance questioned against the service standards, sometimes feedback from the team is revealed as to why they are not following the process. They may have already picked up challenges in the processes and created their own workarounds. This whole process helps to get those conversations on the table and resolve the elephants in the room that the staff see, but that the management may not.

These emotional experiences as a whole provide depth to the story. The lows will indicate processes that are not working or have issues, and highlight the areas for focused improvement. Alternatively, the highs will indicate the points of positive engagement and satisfaction that need to be repeated and made a part of the process. This leads towards change that aims to maximise positive experiences based on repeatable processes, while being able to compare the delivery of those services between the different individual styles.

When a specific individual's style is found to excel over others, the nuances of what they do become important refinements to the process for others to follow. These individual team members become a subject to model, to find out what specifically they are doing that increases the engagement level and positive experience. On identifying these, the process is then updated and the other team members are trained so that it becomes the new way to do business.

This whole process aims to analyse excellence and identify the formula that can be repeated, independent and beyond any charismatic charm of individual team members. From the analysis, the process is refined and then tested through role-playing, until the improvements are validated and consistent. This is not too dissimilar to how stage comedians operate. If anyone attended their performances night after night, they would come to realise how practiced their performances are. Those seemingly accidental slips on the stage, the body noises, the sudden loss of memory . . . the list goes on. They try, test, alter and continue this refinement process until their routine works. There is a cycle of continuous improvement and what appears so natural is a practiced routine.

Try the example of coming up with an elevator speech – that 30-second talk gives an introduction to the business to other people. A good elevator pitch is refined enough to make sure it comes across with confidence and ease and makes sense as a key message in itself. It needs to roll off the tongue, providing enough clarity as to what the company does, with enough mystery to get them asking for more. Once the elevator speech is practiced enough, it will show in the speaker's confidence level, and then they are ready for live testing.

The live test phase is where the new refined process is tested with a real client. Any feedback leads to further refinement and recording. The learning is fed back into the role play and live tested again, until the final version is reached. At this point the team gets the full training. With the elevator speech, this is tested with real people, and then their body language and direct verbal responses are used as feedback, and the speech is refined until it has the desired impact on others. The outcome clients see is the result of this refining process, but there must always be a search for continuous improvement thereafter because, as people change, their needs also alter.

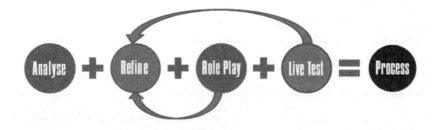

These final processes need to consider the wider impacts on each other, as a change at one step can create a ripple effect on another. This is why roleplay is critical, in order to make sure it works and it has a consistent outcome regardless of the people or environment involved. Fast food franchise operations are a great example. The business systems are so refined that the results are very similar between outlets. This is based on the premise that process guides behaviour, however we are proposing a great process delivered by high-performing people.

We're all regular users of these processes in everyday contexts and it's interesting to see whether it adds or detracts from the experience. Take the example of an interaction with a waiter when making an order in a restaurant. These days, it's common for the order to be taken using a portable digital device. The order can be taken in real time by the waiter while standing next to the customer and, at the same time, the chef receives it in the kitchen. In theory, it increases the efficiency of the whole process as the time-to-order and time-to-table processes are all improved. The waiter then moves to the next customer, and not to and from the kitchen.

The interface with the technology should totally support the people and, if possible, enhance the crucial interaction with the customer. Ideally, manual errors should be removed from the system, so that the technology can eliminate errors like when the waiter is using predefined buttons to select the desired products, yet still needs the flexibility to be able to change customer orders, such as a request to have a different sauce than the one listed on the menu. This means that the format and flexibility of the information displayed for the waiter, and the way the information is presented to the chef, should not disrupt these interactions. Each person involved is a user, and the real gift is in looking at how it enriches each party's life.

Similar questions arise for technology interruptions in the study of the consultation between a medical doctor and the patient. If the doctor is asking questions and concentrating on the technology as they enter information, they may be missing the body language and other important sensory information from the patient. This can break the rapport with the patient in a process where the quality of the relationship is of paramount importance. Using a portable handheld device, instead of a desktop computer, would enable the doctor to observe the patient at the same time and result in a better experience for both.

Testing the interface in terms of when it is used, and how it is used, is important to make sure all benefits are gained and problems eliminated. Ultimately, all business reactions are based on people, and therefore the people and their responses are the key factors for satisfaction.

Technology needs to gain the input, insights and feedback of the users to get early acceptance, while continuing to add innovation that ultimately changes the way they work. Technology must help people interact and reduce human error, and not get in the way of the relationship. In the case of the doctor and patient, technology can be very useful, for instance as software applications can compare pre-inputted historic allergies with prescribed drugs to ensure compatibility. The technology adds value by minimising the risk of human error through the prescription of inappropriate medication, and prevents spelling errors or even missing data.

Technology needs to guide process, and people have to be forward-thinking and innovative enough to see the possibilities of how the two could work together to provide harmonious working relationship.

The key indicator of user satisfaction is the emotional state of the user, not what they may or may not say or do. Don't let a dissatisfied customer walk away without complaining and risk losing them forever.

In this chapter we have focused on the user experience of the customer. However, user experience must also encompass the team members, suppliers, investors, management, government and society. The better the engagement with all these key stakeholders, the more positive the outcomes. It's much easier dealing with a supplier, or indeed any other person, when they are happy. Happy people make any environment more satisfying to be in. Our emotional responses to those around us, and the environments we find ourselves in, influence our state of wellbeing.

Key Lessons

1. The user experience represents a value and emotional based sense of service in relation to the user's engagement with the business.
2. The user experience comprises the business's engagement with prospects, customers, team members, suppliers, investors, board directors, advisors, government and society.

3. The user experience is the expression of a business's DNA, which is the fabric and sum of the business's strategy, values, people, systems, processes, products and services.

4. Touch points are human, auditory, visual, electronic or paper-based interactions between the business and its customers and prospects.

5. The 'user experience emotional analysis' involves capturing emotional responses from touch points, and comparing those events with business expectations, policies, systems, service standards and other codes of conduct.

6. The user experience can be designed and tested internally and externally before becoming standard practice.

7. Continuous improvement in service delivery relates to the process of analysis, refinement, role-playing and live testing.

8. Humanistic businesses are focused on creating consistent positive emotional experiences for their users.

Chapter 13

Contributing to Leaving a Legacy

OVERVIEW
- People want to feel important, respected, valued and to contribute to something bigger than themselves.
- Legacy is not a single act, but the imprints you leave behind in tangible items, or organisational, cultural or sustainable changes to people's lives or thinking.
- A focus on legacy means looking beyond yourself and towards ways of benefiting others.
- There are multiple approaches to creating a legacy.

People desire to be significant, to feel important, to have a sense that they are included and respected and that life counts for something. As we get older and become increasingly aware of our mortality, we come to recognise that we influence and impact others, and that our actions leave imprints on other people.

A great leader understands that every action they take affects the system that they exist within, and that it reflects on, and impacts, the teams they lead. Legacy can be many things, but the greatest legacy that a leader can leave is in the daily acts of genuine concern for the wellbeing of the organisation they lead, and of the people who constitute the organisation. Legacy is not what happens after life, but also during it. The most potent legacy a leader can leave is the way that they have shaped the values, beliefs and experiences of those under their guidance, who in turn influence their own colleagues, families and friends. Beyond their own awareness, their simple small acts can change lives for the better. Though they may never know how.

There's a saying that suggests one should treat everyone with kindness as it's never known if you are entertaining an angel in disguise. The angel here is the gift of learning that each person has through interactions with others, for the benefit of others. Think about the feeling of doing something good for someone else, there is actually a good feeling that always develops within oneself. The irony is that doing good is good for all. Even the concept of karma is about the return of good deeds. We believe that all this is interrelated and that human beings stand alone as a species in how this cycle of giving and receiving works. Giving to one, and often receiving from another.

Perhaps just one person's commitment to live according to a higher set of values can transform the lives of thousands, not necessarily directly, but through the roll-on effect of their acts on others. When a leader demonstrates self-leadership with an open heart in all their relationships, they create a positive force for good. The domino effect of this can continue in the hearts and minds of others, imprinted by a thought or good deed for generations to come. Often it only takes a small group of committed people to create a global impact.

Operating as a humanistic business is all encompassing, from the systems that support the business, to the processes that guide behaviour, and the passion and nuances of the individuals involved. It is truly a holistic approach to engaging, developing, supporting and serving people.

Humanistic business is one of shared values combined with positive intent, passion and purpose, and the desire to connect and create productive relationships. It is through this human interaction that we truly find a place in the world. We see a way to contribute and a way to make best use of our natural gifts and talents. It is not necessarily that our purpose in life is one Holy Grail accomplishment, career contribution, position or event, rather that it is evolving to a point where we connect deeply with people openly, respectfully, purposefully and with integrity. It is a place of service over self and, interestingly, of openly receiving the gifts of others.

Applied to a business context, this concept of service can be seen in negotiations with mutually beneficial outcomes, sponsorship of the needy, mentoring or even business transactions that help others in difficult times. Fast food pioneer McDonald's struggled in its early life, and it's said that the payment terms Coca-Cola gave to the restaurateur helped the cash flow and saved the business. Today Coca-Cola has its biggest client in on-tap soda in McDonald's, and they have a loyal customer because of it. This came about because Ray Kroc approached them with a vision and a call for help, and Coca-Cola smartly lent a hand.[1]

We cannot be leaders where there are no followers, yet we can practice self-leadership at all levels. We cannot become an expert where expertise is not needed or recognised by others, yet we can strive to excel in everything we do. We cannot create world change without first mastering the skills to influence others, just as we cannot feel the full extent of love when we ourselves are not feeling loved. Love is the strongest of human emotions, with its opposite force found in fear. Both are powerful drivers and in their application have very different outcomes and impacts on others. Each fibre of our human being-ness is linked to other people, and the service of others is our greatest opportunity to make sure love is our chosen force.

Our mortality becomes more recognisable as we age. As our health deteriorates, we come to understand the limits of the human body and to better recognise the path to death. This ageing process naturally allows us to question our existence, our purpose and our destiny. While these very things occupy less space in the minds of the young, their importance grows as we grow.

Too many people die after a life of regrets, having not tried hard enough to accomplish their goals, not reaching high enough, not leaving a positive imprint on the hearts of others, and some even having no goals at all. Goals make life meaningful, and a purpose is just another name for a goal. Soon our finite moments on earth seem apparent and we become increasingly concerned with making our life more purposeful. We desire to contribute more, and to be remembered by many. It is not the days that are counted, or the years of our life that matter, rather it is the quality of the life we led that counts, and the imprints we left behind.

Leaving a legacy may not be limited to tangible items; it can be the happiness, the love, the kind gestures that we leave as impressions on others' hearts. It is the love, respect and admiration of others that we have shown, and our genuine efforts in connecting and adding value to one another. A legacy simply means a characteristic mark that lasts beyond our own lives. It can be in many forms, from a business that we started or grew, an activity that was funded by us, a role that served and touched others, a deed that is impacting and guiding the behaviour of another, a friendship that has had a significant influence of another, the parenthood of a child, a physical structure or product, a film or other work of art or images on a book or film.

Establishing and operating a humanistic business often encompasses many of these opportunities. As leaders we face the important question of what influence have we had, and what mark have we left on the hearts and minds of those we have had the privilege to guide and lead. The imprint is not necessarily a significant event, but could be all the small things and previous moments that have a lasting impression. Sometimes we are oblivious to the wake left behind as we busily carry on with our own lives. Our professional responsibilities may be leading an entire organisation or managing a single team, but the fundamental principles of our roles as leaders remain similar. Are we reassuring people about the future? Have we confidently developed a plan to strategically and securely move the organisation forward towards sustainable success and financial security? Has a positive environment been developed so people can thrive and succeed? Am I making a difference?

If leaders are worth remembering, they go beyond the requirement for personal significance and importance, and acknowledge and centre their focus on the betterment of the teams or organisations they lead. When this is accomplished, they establish a legacy that creates a lasting impact which benefits the people they serve. When the CEO departs and the culture they created and nurtured lives on, then they truly achieved a remarkable influence over that organisation and its people.

If a leader is preparing for succession, then much of their energy requires to be directed towards assisting their successor and teams to adjust to the change through the passing of their knowledge and expertise in an effortless manner to the successor. The objective is to create a transition that is seamless and supportive from conception to the first day of the successor's new role, and maintaining and building upon that foundation. When the successor then takes the business to a higher level, the foundation was proved to be strong.

The Values-driven Conversation

Change is an area of great sensitivity for many people. Some fear the uncertainty, and others fear that the good work done to date will be lost. Yet some even fear success. It is a condition of being afraid and it has its power within the unknown it presents, which can be overcome when the leader provides clarity on the future and defines the next steps in the change process. Clarity brings a sense of certainty, predictability, optimism and hope.

Having a powerful impact on teams means recognising that they need both clarity and a sense of importance. When people are included, leaders are giving them that sense of value and importance. Through holding authentic conversations that address their concerns about any change, it opens up the communication with honest and direct dialogue about the future and vision. This form of transparency allows the opportunity for any real or perceived issues to be identified and worked through.

As we discussed earlier, the reality of the human being is that in the absence of information, people will often make up their own story. In the presence of information, people will seek differing levels of detail. But when they feel they have clarity, and they see the management acting on their promises, then trust is built and confidence increases. Uncertainty turns to certainty as people move towards the goal. This is where risks are conquered and a sense of achievement builds. When management does not act according to the methods they themselves promoted, then unpredictability in their actions leads to loss of confidence in them as leaders and trust can be destroyed.

Sometimes it takes leaders to let go of their ownership of their ideas to allow others to contribute and progress the ideas. They become one of the contributors, and don't seek credit for the idea. In fact, the process of letting go sees a transformation from my idea to our idea. It becomes part of the team's focus.

Exhibit Emotional Control

A great leader will transfer knowledge with grace and a willingness to share out of respect for the team members. They will remain transparent in the transfer of their intellectual equity to a successor. This allows them to remain instrumental in creating an environment of cooperation for the seamless transition of responsibilities.

They will do their best to fortify the relationship between the new leader and the existing teams, as well as help create solid relationships between stakeholders, suppliers and staff alike. It becomes important that the transitioning leader recognises and honours their own emotions during the closure, noting that there will always remain human emotions involved in any change. When the transitioning leader remains true to their values and demonstrates congruent focus on the larger picture and vision for the team or organisation, they will create a lasting impact for the betterment of the people they lead and the legacy they will be known for.

As a transitioning leader, there are certain acceptable protocols they are required to follow, in order to leave their professional responsibilities in a better position than when they entered their leadership position.

Each person is defined by the actions they perform in their relationships in both personal and professional life. Success comes in a myriad of forms. For some it will remain in their stature and material possessions, for others it is their children or the lives they have helped transform. There is no correct answer or one that is better than the other. It is a personal choice and normally a response to the individual's values and belief systems.

Establishing a Powerful Legacy

Ultimately, to leave a personal legacy that feels satisfying, each person requires deep self-awareness of personal values that guide individual decision-making processes. Legacy is not something at the end of a career or in preparation for passing over this life, but the identification and acknowledgement of the type of legacy we individually choose to leave.

Personal legacy is the culmination of each person's collective thoughts and actions, and how congruently each has demonstrated their values for the greater success and good of family, staff, stakeholders and customers. Here are four attributes of establishing a powerful legacy:

1. **Be Purposeful** – identify a purpose greater than oneself to help guide energy and resources. People become inspired when they move towards a goal that is bigger than themselves and that aligns with their personal values. To truly make an impact beyond oneself, the benefits must be for a wider key stakeholder group.

2. **Be Excellent** – strive for excellence in word, thought and action. Be committed to remaining congruent and having integrity even when no one is watching. One person's consistent integrity can inspire an entire team to strive for a similar mark of excellence and shine through many difficult situations based upon the will to be great rather than mediocre. By setting an example of personal excellence, one can inspire others and change lives. Become one of the people committed to live differently, work differently and lead differently. Become part of a force so powerful it can change lives just by purposeful intent and will.

   'What makes you think that a small group of committed people cannot change the world for in fact it is the only thing that ever has.'[2]

   Margaret Mead

3. **Be Ecological** – consider decisions and their wide-reaching influences on all the people and aspects of the business that will be affected. Have a genuine concern for all people being impacted by your choices and decisions. Leaders often look for quick solutions to problems without seeing the long-term effects that these solutions will bring. They often don't realise that complex problems need differing perspectives and multiple people involved to find a solution.

4. **Invest in Human Equity** – identify and engage the people around you. One of the greatest gifts is investing in human equity by educating the people you serve. Providing the foundation to up-skill and empower your teams so they can grow and thrive through learning is important.

When a business legacy is left that creates an incredible working environment because of a visionary leader, then that leader has generated an impact on the team that will travel with them throughout their lives. People desire to connect, belong, excel and learn as a fundamental human need that, when met, leaves an indelible impression upon them and the lives of their families, while endearing the brand to the public.

There are six basic approaches that help leaders leave a legacy in their business:

Construct Approach – the ability of a leader to establish a set of constructs of reality that can expand team members' thinking which guides process, policy and behaviour.

Purpose Approach – the ability of a leader to align organisational values and vision to a higher purpose endears people to the vision of the organisation and communities they serve. The loyalty to the vision drives innovation and creativity with greater commitment from stakeholders and a willingness to excel for the greater good that the vision serves. This is the heartbeat of brand energy.

Inclusion Approach – the ability of a leader to create a sense of belonging and personal satisfaction in team members so that they feel they are moving forwards rather than stagnating in an endless routine of mediocrity. When a leader invests in their human equity, they send the message, 'I believe in you, I care about you, I desire you to improve your life.'

Development Approach – the ability of a leader to establish an environment for others in which they can learn, grow and develop their individual leadership capabilities.

Innovation Approach – the ability of a leader to drive innovation within the team, which leads to a high market influence through its products and services that often creates new market interest.

Systems Approach – the ability of a leader to see and organise the business as an ecosystem of people, structures and processes that interact with one another to make an organisation 'healthy' or 'unhealthy'.

When these disciplines are enacted within an organisation, a culture of learning evolves from the mind-set of victim and shifts from drone participants in a passionless direction who are adding little value to the staff, to a vibrant learning organisation of accountable leaders directing their destiny through the values, beliefs and larger vision that is driving their organisation.

The ability of each person to create a positive impact on the lives of others, and build a legacy of good, is only limited by a belief in existing capabilities and a lack of strategy. The more one lives in a world ruled by fears, doubts and limiting beliefs, especially of scarcity and struggle, the more fear and contraction will be experienced, both personally and professionally.

Each person's life is reflected in their professional careers and is a profound reflection of how they think, feel and operate in their personal world. Each of us has a choice to create a life and business filled with heart, compassion and integrity, thereby establishing a powerful force for good that has a wide-reaching influence over the people and communities in our lives, and the businesses we serve.

'When we let the expectations of others or our own unreasonable self-expectations rule, we silence the power of our Legacies.'[3]

Joy DeKok

Life and business are a personal creation and demonstrate how each person touches the lives of those with whom they have had the honour to engage. Individual legacy will demonstrate the values each person has lived by, the words spoken, the relationships that have been built and the thoughts and actions that were performed. Legacy is the sum total of how each of us has lived in the world, what will be left behind and how we will be remembered. In order for our personal lives and businesses to develop their soul and practice the principles of humanistic business, they must operate from vision and purpose bound by integrity and wisdom.

In order to build a powerful legacy, it's important to develop a reference point for what would define a meaningful existence. Legacy is built throughout a person's life and when the destination of the legacy is clearly defined, then individual daily actions can be referenced back to the end goals and act as a relevancy check to verify whether behaviour is in alignment with the goal to build a powerful legacy or whether it is missing the mark. Consider the words of Albert Einstein:

> *'Imagination is more important than knowledge. For knowledge is limited to all we now know and understand, while imagination embraces the entire world, and all there will ever be to know and understand.'*[4]

Personal legacy is built day by day, conversation by conversation, relationship by relationship, each one being measured against the congruency of values and personal purpose and how these are demonstrated in daily life. The more heart and soul that is brought to life's engagements, the more influence will be demonstrated within the organisations, families and team relationships that each of us live within daily. As we individually learn to create more congruency between behaviour and the legacy we desire to leave, we create a daily contribution toward the legacy we desire to make. Individual legacy is built through a combination of actions and personal values, congruently demonstrated within the family, with team members, stakeholders and customers. It is a moment by moment choice; to be mediocre or extraordinary.

Humanistically focused businesses are most likely to fulfil those needs and, through their service to others, build and grow sustainable businesses. Bringing together people with clear goals and a strong 'why' is fundamental to success, but in the long term the fundamental need is for shared values and following a greater purpose that will live beyond our self.

As each of us defines a meaningful vehicle to express our contribution there remains evidence that communities around the world require more assistance than ever before. As populations rise, intolerance increases between the differences in ideology, religion and nationalistic pride. Governments globally continue to struggle with supplying food, energy and resources to support their societies. Our world is facing a non-sustainable future with limited insight into how to create greater balance.

Consciously operated organisations can make an enormous contribution to the communities in which they serve. Our intent is to increase awareness and deliver a methodology that transforms capitalism into a powerful force for good. We hope to accomplish this by aligning businesses with systems which simplify the three core elements to success: strategy, people and process, creating organisational wellbeing that pays it forward into communities by demonstrating leadership and endearing humanistic brands that serve communities and loyal customers.

We invite you to join us in the movement to do good in the world, to connect, to respect diversity and engage with a higher purpose and leave a legacy that will continue to make a positive impact for generations to come.

Key Lessons

1. Legacy means leaving an imprint that lasts beyond our own lives.
2. Legacy can be tangible or intangible in nature, such as a lasting effect on an organisational culture, or a sustainable change in a person's life or thinking.
3. Legacy often transcends the need for personal significance and translates to creating a lasting beneficial impact on others.
4. Succession planning is a fundamental principle in leaving a legacy. Provide clarity with open and authentic conversations to address the fear of change so that uncertainty can transform into clarity in the teams you lead.
5. A great leader transfers knowledge willingly and remains transparent in the transferring of intellectual equity to the successor.
6. Our legacy is the culmination of our thoughts, actions and how congruently we demonstrate our values for the greater success of those individuals we engage with throughout our lives.
7. The four keys to leaving a legacy are:

    a. Be purposeful – have a larger purpose greater than yourself;
    b. Be excellent – strive for excellence in your words thoughts and actions;
    c. Be ecological – consider the wide-ranging influences on all people and act out of genuine concern for their wellbeing; and

    d. Invest in people – build the human equity to help people self-lead. Educate them so that the knowledge can benefit their lives in every context.

8. A dynamic legacy is based upon the consideration of the effects of your decisions for years to come.
9. Each person is faced with a choice daily to build a magnificent legacy. That choice is: do I live today and conduct my business filled with heart, compassion and integrity, or do I live this day taking a lower road?

---

[1] Global Environmental Management Initiative http://www.gemi.org/supplychain/E1C.htm

[2] Margaret Mead http://www.brainyquote.com/quotes/authors/m/margaret_mead.html

[3] Kekok, J. quotation: http://www.goodreads.com/quotes/701321-when-we-let-the-expectations-of-others-or-own-unreasonable

[4] Collected quotes of Albert Einstein http://rescomp.stanford.edu/~cheshire/EinsteinQuotes.html

Index